J -Asim

365
Quick Recipes

DUMONT
monte

Copy Editing: APE Overath
Cover photography (left and right): Brigitte Sporrer
and Alena Hrbkova
Cover photography (middle): Christel Rosenfeld

© 2001 DuMont Buchverlag, Köln
        DuMont monte UK, London

ISBN 3-7701-7043-1

Printed in Slovenia

Content

Content (continued)

Baguette-Rolls with Mushroom Butter

1. Cream the butter, then add the diced mushrooms and season with salt and pepper.
2. Spread the mushroom butter on two baguette rolls and garnish with cucumber slices and parsley.

Two servings
10 minutes

100 g (3 1/2 oz) butter
(room temperature)
3 tablespoons diced,
sautéed, mushrooms
salt
pepper
2 baguette rolls
cucumber slices and pars-
ley as garnish

Crispbread with Banana and Bread with Tomato

One Serving
10 minutes

1 slice crispbread
2 tablespoons cottage
cheese
1/2 small banana
2–3 shelled hazelnuts (filberts)
a little honey (optional)

Spread 1 tablespoon cottage cheese on a slice of crispbread. Peel the banana, cut into slices and arrange on the crispbread with cottage cheese. Slice the hazelnuts and place on the banana slices. Add the honey if desired.

3

Carpaccio with Raw Asparagus

Eight servings

10 minutes

8 sticks green asparagus
2 tablespoons lemon juice
salt
freshly ground pepper
5 tablespoons sunflower oil
60 g (2 oz) Parma or similar dried ham
1 bunch rocket

1. Wash the asparagus and remove the woody ends. Cut the asparagus diagonally into slices 2 mm (1/10 in) thick.

2. Mix the lemon juice, salt, pepper and oil to make a marinade. Pour over the asparagus, stir gently and leave to stand for a while.

3. Arrange the ham on four plates and place the marinated asparagus on top.

4. Wash and dry the rocket. Put on top of the asparagus and sprinkle with ground pepper.

Bruschetta

1. Cut the tomatoes into quarters and remove the seeds. Dice the tomato quarters. Coarsely chop the basil and parsley. Peel and chop the cloves of garlic.

2. Mix the herbs and diced tomatoes in a bowl, add the chopped garlic and season with salt and pepper.

3. Toast the slices of white bread and sprinkle with olive oil. Put some of the tomato mixture on each slice of toast. Serve immediately.

Four servings
10 minutes

4 medium tomatoes
1/2 bunch basil
1/2 bunch parsley
1 clove garlic
salt
pepper
8 slices white bread
4 tablespoons olive oil

5 Yoghurt with Fruit

One serving
10 minutes

125 g / 4 1/2 oz (1/2 cup) low fat yoghurt
1 teaspoon maple syrup
1 teaspoon oat bran
50 g / 2 oz (1/5 cup) black-berries
1/2 banana
1 teaspoon lemon juice
1 kiwi fruit
2 tablespoons oat flakes

1. Place the yoghurt, maple syrup and oat bran in a deep bowl and stir well. Wash and dry the blackberries. Peel the banana, cut into slices and sprinkle with lemon juice. Peel the kiwi fruit and cut it into slices.

2. Garnish the yoghurt with the sliced banana and kiwi fruit. Toast the oat flakes without oil in a non-stick pan until light brown. Leave to cool and sprinkle over the fruit.

6

Three-grain Muesli with Butter Milk

One serving
10 minutes

1 tablespoon rolled wheat flakes
1 tablespoon rolled spelt flakes
1 tablespoon rolled barley flakes
1 tablespoon honey pops (puffed wheat, coated with honey)
1 teaspoon raisins
1 teaspoon sunflower seeds
1/2 apple
125 g (4 1/2 oz) butter milk
4–5 hazelnuts (filberts)

1. Place the wheat, spelt and barley in a large bowl and stir well. Add honey pops and raisins.
2. Put the sunflower seeds in a non-stick pan and toast briefly without oil. Allow to cool down and add to the cereal mixture.
3. Peel an apple, cut it in half and remove the core. Grate one apple half finely and add to the cereal mixture. Pour the sour milk over the cereal mixture, stir well and leave to stand for a few minutes. Garnish with the hazelnuts before serving.

1. Rinse (do not clean) the anchovies under running water.

2. Put flour on a plate. Drizzle fish with lemon juice, salt lightly and coat in flour.

3. Heat a large amount of vegetable oil in a casserole, and fry the anchovies. The fish may also be fried in a deep-fryer, if available.

4. Arrange the crispy fried fish on plates and serve with lemon wedges.

Four to six servings
10 minutes

500 g small anchovies
flour
2 tablespoons lemon juice
salt
vegetable oil
1 lemon, organically grown

8 Sautéed Mushrooms

Four to five servings

10 minutes

500 g (17 oz) small field
mushrooms
3 tablespoons lemon juice
100 g (3 1/2 oz) nonsliced
Serrano ham
3 tablespoons olive oil
3 spring onions
3 cloves garlic
salt
pepper
1/2 bunch parsley or a few
thyme sprigs

1. Clean mushrooms from any remaining soil and cut out spots and bruised parts. Quarter and sprinkle with lemon juice.

2. Cut Serrano ham into small cubes. Heat olive oil in a pan and fry ham briefly.

3. Clean spring onions, wash and cut into thin pieces. You may use part of the green stalk as well, as long as it is tender. Peel garlic cloves, chop coarsely and sauté in a pan with spring onions for about 2 minutes.

4. Stir in mushroom quarters and lemon juice, cover and leave to simmer for a few minutes. Check if ready – the mushrooms should be just tender.

5. Season mushrooms with salt and pepper, wash herbs, finely chop and sprinkle over mushrooms. Serve with toasted white bread.

Fresh Cereal Muesli with Raspberries

1. Place the crushed oats in a large muesli bowl, add the apple juice and leave to soak overnight.
2. Place the yoghurt, rosehip purée and grated (untreated) orange zest in a bowl and stir well. Add the crushed oats and stir well again.
3. Add the raspberries to the yoghurt and crushed oats mixture and stir carefully. Sprinkle the sunflower seeds over the muesli.

One serving
10 minutes

2 tablespoons crushed oats
100 ml / 3 1/2 fl oz (1/2 cup) unsweetened apple juice
100 g / 3 1/2 oz (3/8 cup) yoghurt
1 tablespoon honey-sweet-ened rosehip purée
1 pinch grated orange zest
100 g / 3 1/2 oz (1/2 cup) raspberries
1 tablespoon sunflower seeds

10 Hearty Whole Grain Sandwich with Ham Pâté

Two servings
10 minutes

100 g (scant 4 oz) ham
3 1/2 tablespoons butter
1 tablespoon mustard
salt and pepper
2 large slices of a hearty whole grain bread
2 tomatoes, sliced and parsley for garnish

1. Dice the ham finely in a mixer. Cream the butter until soft, then stir in the diced ham. Season with mustard, salt and pepper.
2 Spread the ham pâté on two slices of bread and top with slices of tomato and parsley.

11 Cinnamon Muesli with Raspberries

One serving

10 minutes

3 tablespoons rolled oat flakes
2 pinches cinnamon
1 teaspoon maple syrup
1 tablespoon cornflakes
3 tablespoons low-fat quark
2 tablespoons low-fat milk (1.5%)
1 teaspoon flaked (slivered) almonds
1–2 tablespoons raspberries

1. Put the oats, cinnamon and maple syrup in a deep bowl and stir well. Add the cornflakes and stir again.

2. Pour the low-fat quark and milk into a small bowl, stir until smooth and pour over the cereal mixture. Sprinkle with almond flakes.

3. Wash the raspberries, dry and garnish the muesli with them.

Honey and Ham Toast 12

1. Toast the slices of wholegrain bread until golden brown. Spread low-fat quark on one and top with a little honey.

2. Spread tomato purée on the other piece of toast and garnish with a slice of ham.

One serving

10 minutes

2 slices wholegrain toast
1 tablespoon low-fat quark
1 teaspoon acacia honey or wild honey
1 teaspoon tomato purée
1 thin slice cooked ham

Pear Quark with Crispbread

1. Place the low-fat quark and milk in a bowl and stir to make a smooth mixture. Wash the pear, cut into quarters and remove the core. Cut into very small cubes and stir into the quark.

2. Sweeten the quark with honey and add the spelt flakes. Leave to stand for a few minutes.

3. Pour the pear yoghurt into a small bowl and sprinkle the yeast flakes on top. Serve with crispbread.

One serving
10 minutes

200 g (7 oz) low-fat quark
2 tablespoons low-fat milk (1.5%)
1 pear
1 teaspoon honey
1 tablespoon rolled spelt flakes
1 teaspoon yeast flakes
2 slices crispbread

Pumpkin Seed Bread with Marmalade

One serving
10 minutes

1 slice pumpkin seed bread
1 tablespoon low-fat quark
1 teaspoon marmalade or fruit spread as preferred
1 small orange

1. Spread the low-fat quark on the pumpkin seed bread and cover with the orange marmalade or other reduced-sugar fruit preserve.

1. Peel the clementine or orange and cut into eight pieces. Arrange them with the bread on a plate.

Wholemeal Bread with Herb Quark

One serving

10 minutes

70 g (3 oz) low-fat quark
1 tablespoon milk
freshly ground pepper
1 pinch paprika
sea salt
1 small onion
1/2 bunch chives
2 tablespoons cress
2 slices wholemeal (whole-wheat) bread

1. Stir the low-fat quark and milk in a bowl until smooth. Season with sea salt, paprika and freshly ground pepper.

2. Peel the onion and chop very finely. Wash the chives and chop finely. Wash the cress and dab dry. Chop half the cress finely and stir into the quark with the onion and herbs.

3. Spread the herb quark on the slice of wholemeal bread and garnish with the rest of the cress.

1. Chop the walnuts coarsely. Wash and prepare the berries. Peel the bananas, wash and prepare the pears. Cut the fruit into bite-sized pieces, put it all in a bowl and sprinkle with lemon juice.

2. Fry the spelt flakes briefly in a non-stick pan without any oil. Leave to cool and pour them over the fruit.

3. Stir the honey and cinnamon in a small bowl well to obtain a smooth mixture. Pour over the fruit and spelt flakes. Finally sprinkle the coarsely chopped walnuts over the muesli, and leave to stand for a few minutes.

One serving
10 minutes

1 tablespoon walnuts
1 tablespoon berries (for instance, strawberries or blackberries)
1/2 banana
1/2 pear
1 teaspoon lemon juice
3 tablespoons spelt flakes
1 small carton low-fat yoghurt (1.5%)
1 pinch cinnamon
1 teaspoon honey

17 Breaded Mangel Sticks

Four servings
10 minutes

12–15 mangel sticks
flour
4 eggs
200 g / 7 oz breadcrumbs
olive oil
salt

1. Blanch mangel sticks and dry well.
2. Coat in flour, then in beaten eggs and finally in breadcrumbs.
3. Heat olive oil (2 fingers high) in a cast-iron pan and fry breaded mangel sticks to a golden brown. Season with salt and serve.

Breaded Camembert with Cranberry Jam 18

1. Beat the eggs in a shallow bowl. Sprinkle the flour for breading onto a flat plate. Dip the pieces of camembert first into the beaten eggs and then dredge with flour.
2 Heat the butter in a pan and brown the pieces of camembert until both sides are crispy. Place on four small plates and garnish with a little cranberry jam.

Four servings
10 minutes

2 eggs
flour for breading
4 pieces camembert
1 tablespoon butter
4 tablespoons cranberry jam

Crispbread with Parma Ham

1. Spread fromage frais on 2 slices of wholemeal crispbread and put 2 slices of Parma ham on each one. Wash the basil leaves and dab dry. Garnish the crispbread topped with ham with the basil leaves and season with freshly ground pepper.

2. Arrange the crispbread on a flat dish. Wash the tomatoes, remove the stalk and cut into slices. Arrange the tomato and cucumber slices around the two slices of crispbread.

One serving

10 minutes

2 slices crispbread
2 tablespoons low-fat fromage frais
4 thin slices Parma ham
a few leaves of basil
freshly ground pepper
1–2 small tomatoes
2–3 slices cucumber

20

Bread with Tomato

One serving

10 minutes

1 slice crispbread
2 tablespoons cottage cheese
1 slice wholemeal bread
1 tomato
3 sprigs parsley
salt and freshly ground pepper

1. Spread the cottage cheese on the slice of wholemeal bread. Wash the tomato, remove the stalk, cut into eight pieces and arrange on the bread. Wash the parsley, chop the leaves finely and sprinkle over the tomatoes. Season with a little salt and freshly ground pepper.

21
Nectarine Yoghurt

Two servings
10 minutes

1 ripe nectarine
125 g / 4 1/2 oz (1/2 cup)
low-fat yoghurt (1.5%)
1 tablespoon maple syrup
2 tablespoons oat flakes
1 teaspoon flaked (slivered)
almonds

1. Wash the nectarine carefully, pat dry, remove the stone and purée with a hand-mixer in a tall beaker. Stir in the yoghurt and sweeten with maple syrup.
2. Fry the oat flakes in a non-stick frying pan without oil. Leave to cool briefly and stir into the yoghurt mixture. Serve the nectarine yoghurt in a muesli bowl and sprinkle with almond flakes.

Wholemeal Roll with Turkey
22

1. Cut the wholemeal roll in half and spread diet margarine on both halves. Put a slice of turkey breast on each one.
2. Peel the carrot and cut into thin slices. Wash and prepare the radishes, cut them in half, season with a little salt and arrange the sliced carrot and radish on each half roll.

One serving
10 minutes

1 wholemeal bread roll
1 teaspoon diet margarine
2 slices lightly smoked
turkey breast
1 small carrot
4 radishes
salt

Fromage Frais and Apple Open Sandwich

23

1. Spread the fromage frais on the slice of bread and sprinkle a little paprika on top.
2. Wash the cress and dab dry. Sprinkle the cress and sunflower seeds over the fromage frais.
3. Wash the apple, cut into eight pieces and remove the core. Garnish the bread and fromage frais with the pieces of apple and arrange on a flat platter.

One serving
10 minutes

1 slice wholemeal (whole-wheat) bread
20 g (3/4 oz) low-fat fromage frais
paprika
1 tablespoon cress
1 tablespoon sunflower seeds
1 apple

Toast with Fish Spread

24

Two servings
10 minutes

100 g (scant 4 oz) smoked fish
50 g (3 1/2 tablespoons) butter
1 tablespoon medium-strength mustard
rose paprika
4 slices of bread, lightly toasted
marinated vegetables

1. Debone and finely chop the fish. Cream the butter and then add the chopped fish. Season with mustard and rose paprika.
2. Spread the mixture on the toast and garnish with marinated vegetables.

Tomatoes with Tofu and Basil Dumplings

Four servings
10 minutes

150 g (5 oz) tofu (bean curd)
100 g (3 1/2 oz) curd cheese
2 cloves garlic
2 spring onions (scallions)
10–12 leaves of basil
3 tablespoons finely chopped walnuts
700 g (1 1/2 lb) sliced firm tomatoes
1 tablespoon balsamic vinegar
5 teaspoons olive oil
salt
freshly ground pepper
1/2 teaspoon sugar

1. Crumble the tofu finely and mix with the curd cheese. Peel the garlic and spring onions and chop finely. Wash the basil and pat it dry. Put a few basil leaves aside for the garnish and finely chop the rest. Add the garlic, spring onions, basil and walnuts to the tofu and cheese mixture and stir well. Leave to stand briefly.

2. Wash the tomatoes, remove the stalks, cut into slices and arrange on a dish. Mix together the vinegar, oil, salt, pepper and sugar to make a marinade and pour over the tomatoes. Moisten your hands and roll the prepared mixture into little dumplings. Add them to the tomatoes and garnish with basil leaves.

1. Put tomatoes in a pot, pour boiling hot water over them and leave to soak for a minute. Take out tomatoes, skin, remove stem, cut in half, deseed and pour away juice. Mash tomatoes with a fork. It should not be too juicy.

2. Peel garlic cloves and cut in half. Toast bread slices on grill and rub with garlic halves while still warm. Spread tomato mash on bread, season with salt and pepper. Drizzle one tablespoon of olive oil over each slice of bread.

3. Place two slices of Serrano ham on each piece of bread and garnish with some black olives.

Four servngs
10 minutes

4 Italian tomatoes
2 cloves of garlic
4 slices of hearty brown country-bread
salt
freshly ground pepper
4 tablespoons olive oil
8 thin slices Serrano ham
8 black olives, pickled in brine

Unleavened Bread with Tomatoes and Yoghurt

Four servings
10 minutes

800 g (1 3/4 lb) ripe sweet
tomatoes
2 red onions
1 bunch smooth parsley
500 ml / 17 oz (2 1/4 cups)
yoghurt
sugar
salt
cayenne pepper
paprika
1 tablespoon lemon juice
1 loaf unleavened (matzo)
bread

1. Cut the tomatoes into small cubes and slice the peeled onions wafer-thin. Coarsely chop the parsley.

2. Put the yoghurt in a bowl and stir vigorously with a whisk until smooth. Mix together the diced tomatoes, onion rings, parsley, sugar and seasoning. Add lemon juice to taste.

3. Cut the unleavened bread into 8 slices and cut in half horizontally. Place the bread slices on four plates and cover with the tomato and yoghurt mixture.

Bread with Strawberries

1. Spread fromage frais on the slices of rye bread. Wash the strawberries, dry and remove the stalks. Cut the strawberries into slices and sprinkle with lemon juice.

2. Arrange the strawberries on the bread. Season with ground pepper. Wash the mint leaves, chop finely and sprinkle over the strawberries.

One serving
10 minutes

2 slices wholemeal (whole
grain) rye bread
2 teaspoons low-fat
fromage frais
150 g / 5 oz (1 cup) strawberries
1 teaspoon lemon juice
freshly ground black pepper
2 mint leaves

Prawn (Shrimp) Cocktail with Apples

1. Peel the apples, remove the cores and quarter. Cut the quarters into fine slices. Sprinkle with lemon juice.

2. Wash the prawns, peel and clean. Bring 300 ml/10 fl oz (1 1/4 cups) water to the boil in a small saucepan, add the prawns and cook for 3 to 4 minutes.

3. Remove the prawns from the water and drain. Mix the prawns with the marinated apple slices and spoon into cocktail glasses.

4. For the sauce, mix the cream with salt, pepper, sugar and some dill, add the white wine and stir the whole until smooth.

5. Wash the tomato, cut out the stalk end and slice into decorative thin strips. Pour the sauce over the prawn mixture and garnish with the dill and strips of tomato.

Four servings

15 minutes

350 g (12 oz) apples
juice of 1 lemon
75 g/3 oz (1/2 cup) prawns (shrimps)
100 ml/3 1/2 fl oz (scant 1/2 cup) sour cream
salt
freshly ground white pepper
1 sprinkle of sugar
2 tablespoons dill
20 ml (2 tablespoons) white wine
1 tomato

Shrimp and Artichoke Omelette

Four servings

15 minutes

200 g / 7 oz (1 cup) deep-sea shrimps, peeled and sautéed
2 tablespoons lemon juice
 4 pickled artichokes (timed)
3 tablespoons olive oil
4 eggs
salt
freshly ground black pepper

1. Place deep-sea shrimps onto a plate and drizzle with lemon juice. Drain artichokes well and cut into 8 pieces.

2. Heat olive oil in a coated pan and briefly fry shrimps.

3. Beat eggs with salt and freshly ground pepper and pour slowly over shrimps. Leave to thicken for about 2 minutes.

4. Place artichoke pieces on omelette and leave for another 3 minutes. Turn omelette out with the help of a plate. Bake on other side for 5 minutes. Slide it carefully onto a plate and cut like a cake. Serve hot and with some lightly toasted white bread rubbed with garlic.

Fried Green Tomatoes with Béchamel Sauce

1. Slice the green tomatoes. Beat the eggs.

2. Pre-heat the oven to its lowest setting, 80 °C (175 °F), gas mark 1. Heat the clarified butter in a large saucepan.

3. Dip the tomato slices first in the beaten eggs, then in the breadcrumbs. On a medium heat, carefully fry the breaded tomato slices a few at a time until golden brown. Season with salt and pepper, arrange on a baking sheet lined with kitchen paper and place in the oven to keep warm.

4. For the sauce: melt the butter in a saucepan and add flour. Stir vigorously with a whisk and slowly add the milk while stirring. Season with salt, pepper, nutmeg and Tabasco. Remove the saucepan from the heat and when it is no longer boiling, stir the egg yolk into the sauce.

5. Put the tomatoes on individual plates and serve the hot sauce separately.

Four servings

15 minutes

6 soft green tomatoes
(already showing traces of orange)
3 eggs
50 g (4 tablespoons)
clarified butter
1–2 cups breadcrumbs
salt
pepper
65 g (5 tablespoons) butter
6 tablespoons flour
500 ml / 17 fl oz (2 1/4 cups)
milk
nutmeg
Tabasco
1 egg yolk

32

Green Tomatoes with Cucumbers

Four servings

15 minutes

6 large green tomatoes
(already showing some
traces of orange)
1 cucumber
butter and oil for frying
1–2 cups condensed milk
1–2 cups fine porridge
(rolled) oats
salt
pepper

1. Pre-heat the oven at its lowest setting, 80 °C (175 °F). Cover a baking sheet with kitchen paper.

2. Cut the tomatoes and peeled cucumber into slices 1 cm / 3/8 in thick.

3. Heat equal amounts of butter and oil in a large frying pan

4. Dip the tomato and cucumber slices in condensed milk and coat on both sides with rolled oats. Carefully fry a few at a time on both sides until the vegetables begin to turn brown.

5. Place the fried tomatoes and cucumbers on the baking sheet and put in the oven to keep warm. Season with salt and pepper before serving.

Hard Boiled Eggs with Mayonnaise

33

1. Beat the egg yolks with a pinch of salt. Add the oil drop by drop, beating continuously until the mayonnaise is completely stiff. Season with a bit of lemon juice and salt to taste.

2. Halve the hard-boiled eggs lengthwise, garnish with the mayonnaise and top with a little of chopped parsley.

Four servings
15 minutes

2 egg yolks
salt
1/8 l (1/2 cup) oil
lemon juice
4 hard-boiled eggs
parsley, freshly chopped

34

Quark with Crunchy Cereal Flakes

One serving
15 minutes

150 g (5 oz) low-fat quark
1 teaspoon vanilla sugar
2 tablespoons milk
1 tablespoon wild honey
2 tablespoons mixed cereal flakes
1 tablespoon grated coconut

1. Place the quark in a bowl with vanilla sugar and milk and stir to make a smooth mixture.

2. Heat the honey in a small non-stick pan, add the mixed cereals and fry until golden brown, stirring continuously. Remove the pan from the heat, leave the honey and cereal mixture to cool down, then pour over the quark. Sprinkle grated coconut on top.

Tapa à la Musa

Three servings

15 minutes

500 g / 17 oz (2 1/2 cups)
chicken hearts
2 cloves garlic
5 tablespoons of extra virgin
olive oil
salt
black pepper, freshly ground
1/2 teaspoon dried rosemary
2 teaspoons of lemon juice

1. Bring water to the boil and simmer the chicken hearts for about 10 minutes. Drain well.

3. Chop the garlic and sauté in 3 tablespoons of oil for 2 minutes. Add the chicken hearts and brown for two minutes.

3. Put the mixture into a small bowl and season with salt, pepper and rosemary to taste. Add the rest of the olive oil and sprinkle with lemon juice. Mix well.

Tomato Omelette with Basil and Goat Cheese

1. Peel and quarter the tomatoes; remove the seeds. Dice the tomato quarters into cubes. Melt 15 g (1 tablespoon) butter in a saucepan, add the diced tomatoes and cook gently for 5 minutes. Leave to cool.

2. Beat the eggs with herb salt and pepper in a bowl; stir in the tomatoes.

3. Melt the remaining butter in a pan and make two omelettes from the egg and tomato mixture.

4. Cut the omelettes in half and place on a warm plate. Garnish with basil and sprinkle the goat's cheese on top.

Four servings

15 minutes

3 firm tomatoes
30 g (2 tablespoons) butter
5 eggs
herb salt
freshly ground pepper
6 leaves fresh basil
80 g (3 oz) goat's cheese, crumbled

Scrambled Egg
with Celery on Bread

One serving

15 minutes

1 egg
salt
freshly ground pepper
1/2 bunch chives
1 teaspoon sunflower oil
1 slice wholemeal (whole-wheat) spelt bread
1 teaspoon diet margarine
1/2 stick celery with leaves

1. Beat the egg in a bowl using a whisk and season with a little salt and pepper. Wash the chives, chop finely and add to the beaten egg.
2. Heat the oil in a small non-stick pan, add the egg and allow to thicken for a few minutes over a low flame, stirring with a fork.
3. Spread diet margarine on a slice of wholemeal (wholewheat) spelt bread. Remove the celery leaves, wash and put to one side. Wash the celery stick, cut into very thin slices and arrange on the bread. Serve on a plate with the scrambled egg and garnish with the celery leaves.

Fried Grated Potatoes with Apples

1. Wash the apples thoroughly, remove the cores and quarter. Finely dice.

2. Melt the butter over a medium heat. Add the diced apple and stir into the butter. Add lemon juice, sugar and cinnamon and simmer over a low heat, stirring continuously until the apples are soft and golden brown. Remove from the pan and place in a bowl.

3. Peel the onion and chop finely. Wash and peel the potatoes, grate them with a cheese grater, wrap in a clean tea towel and press out the liquid. Place the onions in a bowl with the potatoes and season with salt and pepper.

4. Heat oil in a large frying pan. Carefully drop in spoonfuls of the potato and onion mixture, press flat and fry for about 6 minutes, turning occasionally. Remove from the pan and drain on kitchen paper.

5. Wash parsley and finely chop.

6. Place a tablespoonful of the caramelised apple mixture on each potato cake. Garnish with sour cream and parsley.

Four servings

20 minutes

250 g (8 oz) untreated eating apples
4 tablespoons butter
1 teaspoon lemon juice
1 teaspoon sugar
1 shake of cinnamon
1/2 onion
2 floury potatoes
salt
freshly ground black pepper
oil
1/2 bunch parsley for garnishing
50 ml / 2 fl oz (1/4 cup) sour cream

39

Tomatoes Stuffed with Asparagus, Eggs and Salad

Four servings
20 minutes

2 eggs
1 tin asparagus pieces
(150 g; 5 oz)
1 tin peas (150 g; 5 oz)
8 beef tomatoes
salt
8 spring onions (scallions)
250 g (9 oz) pork sausage
meat
5 tablespoons yoghurt
3 tablespoons mayonnaise
1 dash lemon juice
sugar
cayenne pepper
paprika

1. Hard-boil an egg, allow to cool and shell.
Cut the asparagus and peas.
2. Cut the top off each tomato and carefully
remove the flesh with a teaspoon. Sprinkle salt
inside the hollowed-out tomatoes.
3. Cut the spring onions (scallions) into slices
about 1 cm (3/8 in) thick. Dice the pork
sausage, chop the eggs, cut the asparagus into
small pieces, add the peas and stir. Add the
dressing (see below). Fill the tomatoes with the
mixture and put the top back on.
4. For the dressing: mix the mayonnaise and
yoghurt to make a smooth mixture. Add
lemon juice and season with salt, sugar,
cayenne pepper and paprika. Pour part of the
dressing onto the salad stuffing and serve the
rest separately.

1. Cut off rind from belly fat and dice fat into 2 cm (1 in) cubes.

2. Heat an iron or frying pan and fry fat cubes at low heat. Stir often to prevent them from sticking to the pan. When pork cracklings are crisp and golden brown, take them out of melted lard with a skimming ladle.

3. Place pork crackling on a plate and season with salt and freshly ground pepper. If you wish, sprinkle with lemon juice as well. Serve with country bread and some red wine.

Six servings

20 minutes

1 kg (34 oz) pork belly fat
salt
freshly ground pepper
a little lemon juice

Hard-Boiled Eggs
with Tartar Sauce

Four servings

20 minutes

2 egg yolks
salt
125 ml / 4 fl oz (1/2 cup) oil
lemon juice
1 onion
green pepper
1 teaspoon capers
1–2 anchovy fillets,
chopped
4 hard-boiled eggs
freshly chopped parsley

1. Beat the egg yolks with a pinch of salt. Add the oil drop by drop and continue stirring until the mayonnaise is thoroughly stiff. Season with a little lemon juice and salt to taste.

2. Chop the onion, green pepper and capers finely and add to the mayonnaise. Mix in 1 or 2 anchovy fillets, finely chopped.

3. Halve the eggs lengthwise and garnish with the mayonnaise. Sprinkle with finely chopped parsley before serving.

1. Remove cheese rind and dice cheese into 2 cm/1 in cubes.

2. Beat eggs with cream and pour into a bowl. Mix cornmeal with finely ground almonds and pour into a small bowl. Put flour into a shallow dish.

3. Roll cheese cubes in flour first, then coat with beaten eggs and finally with the mixture of cornmeal and almonds.

4. Heat olive oil in a large pan and fry cheese cubes until golden brown. Drain on kitchen paper and serve hot.

Four servings

20 minutes

400 g (14 oz) Spanish Manchego, medium hard to hard
2 eggs
1 teaspoon cream
cornmeal
50 g / 2 oz (1/3 cup) almonds, finely ground
flour
250 ml / 8 fl oz (1 cup) olive oil

43 Codfish Croquettes

Four servings

20 minutes

350 g (12 oz) cod fillets
2 tablepoons lemon juice
3 teaspoons Crème Fraîche
2 cloves garlic
1 scallion
1 dried bread roll
2 eggs
salt
2 teaspoons capers
1 tablespoon chopped parsley
1 tablespoon chopped dill
1 tablespoon chopped thyme
freshly ground white pepper
breadcrumbs
olive oil
1 lemon, organically grown

1. Wash fish fillets, pat dry with kitchen paper, cut into pieces, drizzle with lemon juice and purée with Crème Fraîche in blender.
2. Peel garlic cloves and scallions, and chop finely. Crumble dry bread roll coarsely and add together with garlic to fish mixture. Beat eggs, season with salt and carefully fold in with a fork.
3. Chop capers finely and add to mixture along with with herbs and pepper. Wet hands with cold water and form croquettes that are about 8 cm long and 4 cm thick.
4. Coat croquettes in breadcrumbs. Heat sufficient olive oil in a pan and fry croquettes over medium heat until golden brown. Cut lemon into 8 wedges and serve with croquettes.

Chickpeas in Tomato Sauce

1. Heat olive oil in a large saucepan and fry fennel seeds over low heat.

2. Pour boiling water over tomatoes, skin, remove stem, peel and quarter. Add to fennel seeds in pan. Drain cooked chickpeas well and add. Leave to simmer uncovered for 5 minutes.

3. Drain pumpkin chunks and add to tomatoes and chickpeas. Season to taste with salt, pepper, chilli powder, cinnamon and sugar and leave to thicken for about 5 minutes. The sauce should glaze a little and should not be too liquid; if necessary, allow a few minutes more of cooking.

4. Wash mint and parsley and chop leaves coarsely. Fold herbs into sauce, leave to stand briefly and serve warm. A hearty country bread goes well with it.

Four servings

20 minutes

5 tablespoons olive oil
1 teaspoon fennel seeds
250 g (9 oz) tomatoes
250 g (9 oz) chickpeas, cooked (tinned)
150 g (5 oz) sweet-and-sour pickled pumpkin
salt
pepper
a large pinch of hot chilli powder
2 large pinches of cinnamon
1 teaspoon sugar
10 fresh mint leaves
1/2 bunch flat leaf parsley

45

Lamb Chops with Olives

Four servings

20 minutes

4 lamb chops
salt
freshly ground pepper
3 tablespoons olive oil
2 tablespoons sherry
2 tablespoons grape vinegar
100 g (3 1/2 oz) black olives,
without stones
8 fresh mint leaves

1. Wash lamb chops, pat dry with kitchen paper, season with salt and pepper. Heat olive oil in a pan and fry chops from both sides over a brisk heat.

2. Pour sherry and grape vinegar over chops, slice olives finely, add to pan and leave to simmer over a low heat for 5 minutes.

3. Dice half of the mint leaves and add to cooking sauce. As soon as some liquid has evaporated place lamb chops with olive sauce on plates and garnish with remaining mint leaves.

1. Wash and rinse the herring fillets and place in a bowl or deep dish.

2. Wash the apples thoroughly, remove the cores and quarter. Grate the apples, put in a bowl and mix with the horseradish.

3. Crush the bay leaf and the peppercorns, mix with the sour cream and the milk and add to the apple and horseradish mixture. Stir well.

4. Pour over the herrings and serve with brown bread or toast.

Four servings
20 minutes

8 fillets of salted herring
500 g (1 lb) unsprayed apples
1 tablespoon horseradish
1/2 bay leaf
4 peppercorns
250 ml / 8 fl oz (1 cup) sour cream
375 ml / 13 fl oz (1 1/2 cups) milk

47

Scallops in Garlic Sauce

Four servings

20 minutes

1 kg (34 oz) scallops
5 cloves of garlic
1 spring onion
5 tablespoons olive oil
1 red chilli
200 ml / 7 fl oz (7/8 cup) white wine
2 tablespoons lemon juice
2 tablespoons basil, finely chopped

1. Wash and scrub scallops thoroughly with a kitchen brush under running water. Never use scallops that are already open.

2. Peel garlic cloves and spring onion, chop finely and braize in olive oil. Add chilli. Pour white wine and 125 ml (4 fl oz) of water into the pan. Add lemon juice and basil.

3. Bring stock to boil. Place scallops in it, cover and leave to simmer over low heat for 10 minutes. Stir once or twice to ensure even cooking of scallops.

4. Discard any scallops that did not open while cooking – they are inedible. Serve hot scallops in their sauce, together with fresh white bread.

Tortillas Stuffed with Peppers and Sweet Corn

1. Clean the pepper, remove the stalk and seeds and cut into fine strips. Peel the onion and chop finely. Heat the olive oil in a non-stick pan and the fry pepper for about 5 minutes.

2. Drain the sweet corn, add to the pan and heat up briefly. Season the vegetables with salt, cayenne pepper and thyme.

3. Heat the tortillas in the oven for a few minutes following the instructions on the packet and remove from the oven. Place the vegetables on the hot tortillas and roll them up.

Two servings
20 minutes

1 small sweet pepper
1 small onion
1 teaspoon olive oil
100 g / 3 1/2 oz (1/2 cup) sweetcorn (from the tin)
salt
cayenne pepper
some dried thyme
2 tortillas

49

Mozzarella Parcels with Bacon and Tomatoes

Four servings

20 minutes

4 packs mozzarella
(200 g; 7 oz each)
50 g (2 oz) dried tomatoes
2 shallots
1 teaspoon dried basil
4 thin slices streaky bacon
3 tablespoons basil-infused oil
white pepper

1. Let the mozzarella and sun-dried tomatoes drain thoroughly on kitchen paper. Chop the shallots and tomatoes finely. Cut each piece of mozzarella in half horizontally.

2. Pre-heat the oven to its highest setting, 250 °C (480 °F), gas mark 8.

3. Cover each half piece of mozzarella with some chopped shallots and tomatoes. Sprinkle with basil and cover with the other half piece of mozzarella. Wrap each mozzarella parcel with a slice of streaky bacon.

4. Pour some basil oil into an ovenproof dish and put the mozzarella parcels in it next to each other. Place under the grill for about 5 minutes.

5. Just before serving, sprinkle the mozzarella parcels with basil oil and add some white pepper.

Fried Tomatoes with Mint Sauce

1. Cut the plum tomatoes lengthways into slices 1 cm (1/2 in) thick. Season with salt and leave to stand for about 15 minutes.

2. Heat the oil in a pan, add the tomato slices, a few at a time, and fry on both sides until golden brown. Keep warm.

3. For the sauce: pour the yoghurt into a large bowl and stir until smooth. Add the remaining ingredients, stir again and season to taste.

4. Serve the sauce separately from the tomatoes.

Four servings

20 minutes

8 plum tomatoes
salt
olive oil for cooking
500 g / 17 oz (2 1/4 cups) yoghurt
1 tablespoon curry powder
1 pinch ground cinnamon
1 tablespoon chopped fresh mint
1 tablespoon lemon juice
pepper
cayenne pepper

51

Spicy Hard-boiled Egg Spread

One serving
20 minutes

1 egg
1 tablespoon low-fat salad cream
1 tablespoon low-fat quark
1 teaspoon lemon juice
1 small pickled gherkin
1 anchovy fillet (from the tin)
1 pinch chilli powder
freshly ground pepper
1/2 bunch chives
1 wholemeal (wholewheat) roll

1. Hard-boil the egg, peel and cut into half. Leave to cool, then chop finely. Put the low-calorie salad cream, low-fat quark and lemon juice in a bowl and stir well. Carefully fold in the finely chopped hard-boiled egg.

2. Drain the pickled gherkin and anchovy fillet, chop finely and add to salad cream and egg mixture. Season with chilli powder and pepper.

3. Wash the chives, finely chop and add to the salad cream and egg mixture. Arrange on a plate and serve with a slice of wholemeal (wholewheat) bread.

1. Peel the onion and chop finely. Mix in a bowl with the steak tartare, minced meat, egg, breadcrumbs and raisins. Season well with salt and pepper.

2. Form the meat mixture into little balls, heat the oil in a frying pan and fry for 5 minutes. Remove from pan and keep warm.

3. Dice the bacon coarsely and fry in the hot pan until golden brown. Remove from the pan and keep warm.

4. Wash the apples thoroughly, remove the cores and quarter. Cut a quarter of one apple into thin slices and set aside for decoration. Cut the rest of the apples into chunks. Heat the butter and a little sugar in a pan and sauté the apple cubes. Season with salt and paprika.

5. Push the meatballs, bacon and apple cubes alternately onto the skewers and arrange on the plates. Garnish with slices of apple and sprinkle with lemon juice.

Four servings

25 minutes

1 small onion
125 g (4 oz) steak tartare
125 g (4 oz) minced (ground) meat, pork and beef mixed
1 small egg
1 tablespoon breadcrumbs
2 tablespoons raisins
salt
freshly ground white pepper
4 tablespoons oil
100 g (3 1/2 oz) piece of bacon
250 g (8 oz) untreated apples
20 g (1 1/2 tablespoons) butter
sugar
1 teaspoon sweet paprika
4 kebab skewers

53 Grilled Peppers

Four servings

25 minutes

100 g (3 1/2 oz) mild green
peppers
100 g (3 1/2 oz) mild red
peppers
coarse sea salt
a few basil leaves

1. Preheat oven to 200 °C (400 °F), gas mark 6. Rinse green and red peppers and put on grill.

2. Roast peppers for about 20 minutes in oven, take them out and sprinkle with coarse sea salt.

3. Garnish grilled peppers with basil leaves and serve while still hot.

Baked Parmesan Tomatoes

1. Pre-heat the oven to 200°C (400°F), gas mark 6. Grease a baking sheet generously with oil.

2. Using a knife, make a cross-shaped incision 0.5 cm/under 1/4 in deep in the base of the tomato (the opposite end to the stalk). Put the tomatoes next to each other on the baking sheet and bake in the oven for about 15 minutes.

3. Remove the tomatoes from the oven and put a teaspoon of herb butter on the incision of each of the tomatoes. Grate some Parmesan and sprinkle on top of the tomatoes. Now put the tomatoes, topped with Parmesan under a very hot grill for about 5 minutes.

Four servings

25 minutes

oil for the baking sheet
8 beef tomatoes
40 g (3 tablespoons) herb butter
25 g (3 tablespoons) grated Parmesan

Fried Fish

Four servings
25 minutes

300 g (10 oz) fillets of cod or redfish
3 tablespoons lemon juice
salt
2 eggs
3 tablespoons flour
125 g / 4 1/2 oz (3/4 cup) breadcrumbs
250 ml / 8 fl oz (1 cup) vegetable oil for frying
1 lemon
parsley to garnish

1. Rinse fish fillets, pat dry with kitchen paper, slice in half lengthwise and cut across in pieces (approx. the size of a thumb).

2. Place fillets on a plate, drizzle with lemon juice, season with a little salt and leave to soak for 10 minutes.

3. Beat eggs. Prepare three plates for the coating: one with flour, one with beaten eggs, and the third one with breadcrumbs. Pat dry fish pieces with kitchen paper; coat first with flour, then with eggs and finally with breadcrumbs.

4. Heat vegetable oil in a deep-fat frying pan to about 180 °C (350 °F), gas mark 5. Place fish portions into hot oil (it should not be too hot) and fry until crispy. Leave to drain shortly on kitchen paper. Wash lemons and cut into 8 wedges.

5. Serve fried fish on a preheated plate with lemon wedges and parsley leaves.

1. Sift the flour and baking powder together, then stir together with milk, eggs, sugar and a little salt until the batter is smooth. Hints: Let the mixture stand for a while before spooning into the pan to give the flour time to bind the mixture. Your pancakes will be especially light and fluffy if you beat the egg whites separately until stiff and then fold them into the other ingredients immediately before sautéing.

2. Heat a little oil in a frying pan. Pour one ladle of batter into the pan and tip it in all directions to spread the batter evenly.

3. As soon as the bottom of the pancake is golden, turn the pancake with a spatula. Add a bit more oil if necessary.

4. Spread a little jam, honey, Nutella or tinned fruit on top of the finished pancakes and fold them in half.

Four servings
25 minutes

1/2 l (2 cups) milk
1/4 teaspoon baking powder
250 g (2 generous cups) flour
2 eggs
1 teaspoon sugar
pinch of salt
oil for sautéing
jam, honey, Nutella or tinned fruit as topping

Tuna with Courgettes and Peppers

Four servings

25 minutes

1 sweet red pepper
2 courgettes
6 tablespoons olive oil
2 tablespoons pine nuts
salt
freshly ground black pepper
200 g (7 oz) tuna in oil
(tinned)
2 teaspoons fresh, finely
chopped oregano (dried
oregano as an alternative)

1. Wash pepper, quarter and clean. Cut into thin strips.

2. Wash courgettes, remove stem and bud and cut into fine slices.

3. Heat one tablespoon of olive oil in a pan and roast pine nuts over low heat until golden. Remove nuts and set aside.

4. Heat remaining olive oil in pan and quickly fry peppers, add courgettes, cover and leave to simmer for about 10–15 minutes. The vegetables should be just tender. Season with salt and freshly ground pepper.

5. Drain tuna fish well, flake into pieces with a fork, mix with vegetables and simmer briefly. Remove pot from heat, stir in chopped oregano. Place antipasto on plates and sprinkle with roast pine nuts.

Apple and Fish Dip with Curried Sticks

58

1. Wash the smoked mackerel and remove the skin and bones. Put the fish in a blender with the cream cheese and curry powder and blend to a smooth consistency. Season with salt and pepper and place in a small bowl. Set aside.

2. Peel the apples, remove the cores and quarter. Cut the quarters into thin slices and use them to garnish the mackerel paste. Put aside.

3. Pre-heat the oven to 200 °C (400 °F), gas Mark 6.

4. Cut the crust off the slices of bread and put on a baking sheet. Mix the butter and the curry paste together well and spread on the slices of bread.

5. Bake the pieces of bread for about 10 minutes until golden brown and crisp. Cut into sticks and serve with the dip.

Four servings

30 minutes

350 g (12 oz) smoked mackerel
150 g (5 oz) cream cheese
1/2 teaspoon curry powder
salt
freshly ground black pepper
250 g (1/2 lb) apples
4 slices of white bread
25 g (2 tablespoons) softened butter
1 teaspoon Madras curry paste (from supermarkets or Asian shops)

Pork Crackling with Gofio

Four servings

30 minutes

1 tablespoon oats
1 tablespoon spelt (German wheat)
1 tablespoon wheat grain
500 g (17 oz) pork crackling
a pinch of salt
1 tablespoon aniseed liquor
1 tablespoon sugar
1 teaspoon cinnamon
1 teaspoon grated lemon peel, organically grown

1. Roast cereal grains in a pan until golden brown, stirring grains constantly.

2. Knead lard with roast cereals, salt, aniseed, sugar, cinnamon and grated lemon peel. The paste should have a solid consistency, if not, add some more roast grains, taste and season with the spices.

3. Fill sweet-and-spicy paste in a jar which can be closed tightly, and allow to cool. Crumble onto a plate and serve with wine.

Chicken Croquettes

1. Wash chicken breast, pat dry and fry in a pan with a little olive oil for about 8–10 minutes over low heat. Remove and set aside.

2. Melt butter in pan and add 1 tablespoon of finely sifted flour. Stir with a whisk until mixture has thickened.

3. Preheat milk and gradually add to mixture, stirring constantly until a thick Béchamel sauce is obtained. Add salt, freshly ground pepper and nutmeg. Set pan aside.

4. Cut chicken meat into very thin slices or mince in blender and fold with one egg yolk into Béchamel sauce.

5. Beat remaining egg yolk. Use a spoon to form 5–20 equal portions out of croquette mixture, coat in flour, moisturize with both egg whites and beaten egg yolk and roll in cornmeal. Fry in olive oil until golden brown. Wash oregano before serving, strip leaves, chop finely and sprinkle over croquettes.

Four servings
30 minutes

For 15–20 croquettes:
300 g (10 oz) chicken breast
olive oil
15 g butter
2 tablespoons flour
250 ml / 8 fl oz (1 cup) milk
salt
freshly ground white pepper
a pinch of ground nutmeg
2 eggs
cornmeal
1/2 bunch oregano

61

Chicken Breast in Sherry Sauce

Four to six servings

30 minutes

600 g (20 oz) chicken breast, boned and skinned
3 tablespoons lemon juice
flour
3 tablespoons olive oil
freshly ground multi-coloured pepper
250 ml / 8 fl oz (1 cup) dry sherry fino
125 ml / 4 fl oz (1/2 cup) chicken stock
2 cloves of garlic
1 thyme sprig
100 g / 3 1/2 oz (2/3 cup) salted almonds

1. Wash chicken breasts, pat dry with kitchen paper, cut into 3 cm (1 in) cubes and drizzle with lemon juice. Roll chicken pieces on a plate dusted with flour.

2. Heat olive oil in a large saucepan. Divide chicken breasts pieces into serving portions and fry on each side over brisk heat for about 2 to 3 minutes, season with freshly ground multi-coloured pepper, remove chicken from pan, set aside and keep warm.

3. Deglaze the the pan with sherry and fill up with chicken stock. Peel and crush garlic cloves. Add garlic and thyme to sauce. Leave to simmer over medium heat until about one third of the liquid has evaporated.

4. Place chicken breasts in sauce and leave to marmate over low heat for about 10 minutes. Remove pan from heat and add salted almonds. Serve while hot.

Rice Pudding with Mango

1. Pour the milk into a small saucepan and heat slowly. Add the rice and vanilla sugar. Cover and simmer for about 15–20 minutes over a low heat. You can add more milk if necessary. Remove the rice pudding from the heat and leave to cool.

2. Peel the mango and cut into quarters. Then cut the flesh into slices. Pour the rice pudding into a deep bowl and garnish with the mango slices and cinnamon. Finally, sprinkle a few cornflakes on top.

One serving
30 minutes

250 ml / 8 fl oz (1 cup) milk
1 teaspoon vanilla sugar
2 tablespoons round grain (short-grain) rice
1/2 mango
1/2 teaspoon cinnamon
1 tablespoon cornflakes

63

Angel-Food Omelette

One serving
30 minutes

3 eggs
65 g / 2 1/2 oz (generous
1/4 cup) sugar
50 g / 2 oz (scant 1/2 cup)
flour plus a bit more for
dusting the baking form
1 tablespoon jam
icing sugar

1. Separate the eggs and beat the egg yolks with half of the sugar until foamy.

2. Beat the egg whites with the rest of the sugar until stiff. Gently fold in the egg yolk mixture.

3. Sift in the flour and fold it gently under the egg mixture with a whisk.

4. Grease and flour a heatproof baking dish. Pour in the batter and bake at 150 °C (300 °F), gas mark 2, for about 20 minutes. The omelette is done when a knife inserted into the centre comes out dry.

5. Spread jam on the omelette, slip it onto a pre-warmed plate and dust with icing sugar.

Tomato Cocktail with Shrimps and Broccoli

1. Wash and prepare the broccoli and divide into bite-sized pieces. Halve the cocktail tomatoes and put in a large bowl with the broccoli. Cut the ham into fine strips and stir it into the vegetables together with the shrimps.

2. For the salad dressing: whisk the ketchup and herbs vigorously with vinegar. Pour in the oil little by little while continuing to stir, then add the cream. Stir the mixture again until smooth and pour over the salad.

3. Stir the dressing into the salad and leave to stand for about 20 minutes. Stir again just before serving and transfer into four small glass bowls.

Four servings

30 minutes

400 g (14 oz) broccoli
300 g (10 oz) cocktail tomatoes
2 slices cooked ham
100 g / 3 1/2 oz (5/8 cup)
fresh shrimps
2 tablespoons white wine
vinegar
1 tablespoon tomato
ketchup
salt
pepper
6 tablespoons sunflower oil
100 ml / 3 1/2 fl oz (1/2 cup)
cream

Pitta Bread with Chicken and Apple Filling

Four servings

30 minutes

150 g (5 oz) red apples
1/4 red cabbage
2 radishes
1 small red onion
1 tablespoon lemon juice
3 tablespoons low-fat
cream cheese
salt
freshly ground black pepper
200 g (7 oz) cooked chicken
breast without the skin
4 large (or 8 small) pieces of
pitta bread
1/2 bunch parsley for
garnishing

1. Peel the apples, remove the core and quarter. Grate finely.

2. Wash the red cabbage and radishes and cut into thin julienne strips. Peel the onion and cut into fine rings. Put all the ingredients in a large bowl and sprinkle with the lemon juice.

3. Mix in the cream cheese and add salt and pepper to taste.

4. Cut the chicken into bite-size pieces and add to the cabbage mixture.

5. Bake the pitta bread according to instructions. Cut open on one side and fill with the apple, chicken and cabbage mixture.

6. Wash the parsley, chop finely and garnish the filled pitta breads. Serve them while still hot.

Spinach Omelette

1. Wash spinach, remove stems and chop coarsely. Peel potatoes and slice thinly. Heat 4 tablepoons of olive oil in a pan and fry potatoes for about 15 minutes until done. Remove from pan and keep warm.

2. Peel onion and chop finely, seed chilli and chop finely, too. Pour 2 tablespoons of olive oil in a pan and fry onions and chili. Add spinach, sauté for 3 minutes and remove from pan.

3. Beat eggs with salt and pepper, heat remaining oil in pan and leave eggs to thicken briefly, spread mixture of potatoes and spinach over it.

4. Bake omelette at low heat for about 10 minutes in a pan. Slide it carefully onto a serving dish and divide like a cake. Wash chives and chop finely. Garnish with rolls of chives.

Four servings
30 minutes

200 g (7 oz) fresh spinach
3 potatoes
8 tablespoons olive oil
1 onion
1 red chilli
5 eggs
salt
freshly ground black pepper
1 bunch chives

66

Green and White Chequered Cold Cucumber Soup

Four servings
10 minutes

1 large cucumber
1 kg (4 cups) yoghurt
2 tablespoons dried mint
2 cloves garlic, pressed
125 ml (1/2 cup) crushed ice
salt
pepper

1. Slice the cucumber in half lengthwise and take out the seeds. Cut into small pieces and blend in a food processor. Add the yoghurt, dried mint, garlic and ice little by little and blend until the mixture is smooth.
2. Season with salt and pepper and serve immediately.

Chickpea Soup

1. Heat the olive oil in a saucepan and sauté the minced onion until tender.
2. In the meantime, puree the chickpeas with a cup of chicken stock. Add this mixture to the onions with the remaining stock and bring quickly to a boil.
3. Remove from heat, stir in the crème fraîche and season with salt and pepper.

Two servings
10 minutes

2 tablespoons olive oil
1 onion, minced
1 l chicken stock
500 g (2 3/4 cups) chick-peas (tinned)
4 tablespoons crème fraîche*
3 cloves garlic, pressed
salt and pepper

Melon Soup with Marinated Red Ginger

1. Cut the melons in half and remove the seeds. Scrape out the meat and place in a food processor. Little by little mix the melon together with the ice, the ginger, pepper and mint until the mixture becomes fluid.

Four servings

10 minutes

2 ripe honeydew melons
500 ml (2 cups) crushed ice
2 tablespoons ground ginger
1 tablespoon pepper
1/2 tablespoon dried mint

Spicy Watermelon Soup

Four servings

10 minutes

1 ripe watermelon cut in slices, seeds removed
1 tablespoon chili flakes plus a few more for the topping
ice cubes for the platter (as desired)

1. Cut the watermelon meat into pieces and place into the food processor. Save the juice and add to processor!
2. Add the chili flakes and blend briefly. Serve in cooled bowls with ice cubes.

71 Beetroot Soup

Four servings
10 minutes

5 beetroots, cooked and diced
750 ml (3 cups) chicken stock
4 tablespoons crème fraîche*
salt
pepper

1. Place beetroots into the food processor, add a little stock and blend until smooth. Add the remaining stock and mix again. Pour the soup mixture into a pot and bring quickly to a boil. Remove from heat and immediately add the crème fraîche, stirring continuously. Season with salt and pepper.
Serve immediately.

72 Bread Soup

1. Pour the stock into a pot and bring to a boil.
2. In the meantime cut the bread into strips and mince the onion. Heat the butter in a pan and add the bread and onions. Brown briefly until the onions are tender.
3. Add the onions and bread to the stock and simmer together for 2–3 minutes. Add seasonings to taste.

Four servings
15 minutes

1 l (4 cups) stock
250 g (generous 8 oz) bread (use different sorts of bread if possible)
1 onion
30 g (2 tablespoons) butter
salt
caraway seeds
pepper

1. Wash and sort the watercress, dry and chop coarsely.

2. Heat the stock and milk together in a saucepan. Mix the cornflour to a smooth paste with a little cold water and add it to the saucepan using a balloon whisk. Allow to simmer for 5 minutes. Add lemon juice, salt and pepper to taste.

3. Mix the cream with the egg yolks. Peel the hard-boiled eggs and chop them finely.

4. Remove the soup from the heat and thicken with the egg and cream mixture.

5. Place the chopped watercress in soup plates, ladle the soup over it and serve garnished with the chopped egg.

Four servings

15 minutes

1 bunch watercress
750 ml (3 1/2 cups) beef stock
250 ml (1 cup) milk
2 level tablespoons cornflour (corn starch)
juice of 1/2 lemon
salt
freshly ground white pepper
100 ml / 3 1/2 fl oz (1/2 cup) cream
2 egg yolks
2 hard-boiled (hard-cooked) eggs

74 Pea Soup

Four servings

15 minutes

4 tablespoons olive oil
1 large onion, finely
chopped
7 large slices of streaky
bacon, cubed
500 g (3 1/4 cups) fresh
shelled peas
salt
1 l chicken stock
pepper

1. Heat 2 tablespoons olive oil in a frying pan
and add the onion. Sauté until the onion is
tender. Add the bacon and brown until crispy.
Set aside for the time being.
2. Heat the rest of the olive oil in a large pot
and then add the peas and enough water to
cover them well. Add a pinch of salt and boil
for 2–3 minutes until the peas are tender.
3. Place the peas in the food processor and
blend together with 2 cups of the hot stock.
Add the remaining stock slowly and continue
to blend. Season with salt and pepper. Return
to pot and bring the soup once more to a quick
boil.
4. Stir in the bacon-onion mixture and serve.

Green Spring Soup

1. Halve the clove of garlic and rub the saucepan with it. Heat the beef stock in the saucepan.

2. Cut the ham in fine strips and set aside. Wash spinach and remove the stems. Add to the stock and allow to cook over a very gentle heat. Add salt and pepper.

3. Wash and chop the rocambole. Ladle the soup into soup bowls, add strips of ham and rocambole and serve with a fresh baguette.

Four servings

15 minutes

1 clove of garlic
500 ml (2 1/4 cups) beef stock (broth)
100 g (3 1/2 oz) air dried ham
100 g (3 1/2 oz) fresh leaf spinach
salt
freshly ground coloured pepper
several leaves fresh rocambole garlic

Hearty Potato Soup

Four servings

15 minutes

1 1/2 l (6 cups) of beef or vegetable stock
200 g (7 oz) mashed potato flakes
50 g (scant 2 oz) smoked bacon
2 onions
oil for sautéing
salt
pepper
marjoram
rose paprika
savoury
caraway
1 clove garlic
4 thick frankfurters (Bock-wurst or similar)
1 tablespoon butter
fresh parsley

1. Put the stock into a pot and bring to a boil. Stir the mashed potatoes flakes into the hot stock.

2. In the meantime dice the bacon and the onions. Heat oil in a pan and brown the bacon and onion cubes. Add a pinch of salt, pepper, majoram, paprika, savory and caraway.

3. Mince the garlic and add it to the soup together with the bacon and onions.

4. Slice the frankfurters and let them simmer a while in the hot soup.

5. Before serving, add a bit of butter to the soup and garnish with fresh parsley.

1. Hard-boil the eggs, place in cold water and then shell. Mash the yolk with a fork and finely chop the egg white.

2. Add the softened butter and grated cheese to the prepared egg and mix together carefully. Season with a little pepper and salt. If the mixture seems too dry, knead in a little runny egg white.

3. Heat the meat stock. Form little dumplings from the mixture with a teaspoon and add them to the stock. Simmer the cheese dumplings gently, being careful not to let them boil.

Four servings
15 minutes

1 litre (4 1/2 cups) meat stock
2 eggs
20 g (1 1/2 tablespoons) butter
5 tablespoons grated Gruyère cheese
salt
white pepper
egg white

Prawn (Shrimp) Soup

Four servings

15 minutes

2 tablespoons oil
300 g (10 oz) prawns
(shrimps), peeled
200 ml (7/8 cup) madeira
500 ml (2 1/4 cups) fish or
chicken stock (broth)
300 ml / 10 fl oz (1 3/4 cup)
cream
2 egg yolks
salt
freshly ground white pepper
1 tablespoon dill tips

1. Heat the oil in a saucepan and brown the prawns evenly on all sides.
2. Add the madeira and stock and simmer for 2 minutes.
3. Whip 50 ml/2 oz (1/4 cup) of the cream. Separately, beat the rest together with the egg yolks.
4. Remove the soup from the heat and thicken with the cream and egg yolk mixture. Add salt and pepper to taste.
5. Pour into soup bowls and garnish with a dollop of whipped cream and a sprinkling of dill.

Lentil Soup

1. Heat the stock in a pot and bring to the boil.
2. Add the lentils and bacon and let boil for 10 minutes.
2. Remove the bacon and cut into small pieces. Purée the lentils. Return the bacon and lentils to the pot Heat once more and garnish with fresh or dried marjoram before serving.

Four servings
20 minutes

500 g (2 1/2 cups) red lentils
1 l (4 cups) stock
150 g (generous 5 oz)
smoked bacon
salt
marjoram

80 Salsa Mexicana

Four servings
15 minutes

2 tablespoons sunflower oil
200 g (generous 3/4 cup)
tinned who e-kernel corn,
drained
1 shallot, finely chopped
1 red pepper, 1 yellow pepper
2 tomatoes
vegetable stock, as needed
1 teaspoon dried thyme
1 teaspoon dried oregano
salt, peppe

1. Heat the oil in a pan and sauté the corn lightly for five minutes. In the meantime mince the peppers and tomatoes.
2. Add the finely chopped ingredients and stock to the corn and bring to a boil. Simmer for 5 minutes. If the mixture is too thick, add a bit more stock. Season with herbs, salt and pepper.

81 Sorrel soup

Four servings

15 minutes

250 g (8 oz) sorrel
25 g (1 oz) butter
100 ml (1/2 cup) dry white wine
500 ml (2 1/4 cups) veal stock (broth, ready-made)
2 boiled potatoes, peeled
100 g / 3 1/2 oz (1/2 cup) crème fraîche
freshly ground white pepper
salt

1. Wash and sort the sorrel. Dry it and cut into fine strips.
2. Melt the butter in a saucepan. Add two-thirds of the sorrel, all the wine and the veal stock and simmer for 7 minutes. Dice the potatoes and add to the soup. Purée the soup and pass it through a sieve.
3. Stir the crème fraîche into the soup, adding salt and pepper to taste. Re-heat the soup briefly and garnish with the remaining strips of sorrel.

Asparagus Soup with Omelette

Asparagus Soup with Omelette

1. Wash the asparagus and remove the woody ends. Cut into small pieces and simmer gently in salted water with a pinch of sugar for about 10 minutes. Wash the parsley, wipe dry and chop finely.

2. Melt the butter in a large saucepan, add the asparagus and half the parsley. Sprinkle with flour and cook gently. Add the meat stock and simmer over a low heat.

3. Mix together the eggs, egg yolks, cream and flour, season with salt and pepper. Cook the omelette until it is quite firm. Remove from the pan and cut into fine strips. Stir gently into the soup and season with nutmeg. Garnish with parsley.

Four servings

15 minutes

1.5 kg (3 lb) green asparagus
salt
1 pinch sugar
1 bunch parsley
60 g (4 tablespoons) butter
1 tablespoon flour
1.5 litres (7 cups) meat stock (broth)
finely grated nutmeg

For the omelette:
2 eggs
yolks of 2 egg
125 ml / 4 fl oz (1/2 cup) cream
3 tablespoons flour
salt
freshly ground pepper

Porcini and Tortellini Soup

Four servings

15 minutes

4 small firm porcini
2 shallots
1 tablespoon butter
1 litre (4 1/2 cups) beef
stock (broth)
150 g (5 oz) fresh tortellini,
filled with cheese
1 bunch chervil

1. Wash the porcini and cut into fine slices. Cut the slices into tiny cubes. Peel the shallots and finely chop.

2. Melt the butter in a large saucepan, cook the shallots gently until transparent, add the mushrooms and sauté.

3. Pour in the beef stock and simmer for 2 minutes. Add the tortellini and cook in the stock for 5 minutes. They should still be firm to the bite. Wash and finely chop the chervil, adding it to the hot soup. Serve in large soup plates.

Zuppa Pavese (Meat Soup with Egg and Bread)

1. Cut the stale bread into slices 1 1/2 cm / 3/4 in thick and dribble a little milk over them.

2. Put the slices of bread on a lightly greased baking sheet. Beat the eggs. Pour a little of the mixture over each piece of bread. Season with salt and pepper and sprinkle a little parmesan on top. Immediately put into an oven pre-heated to 200°C (400°F), Gas Mark 6, and bake for 5–10 minutes until the egg is set.

3. Heat the meat stock, pour into large soup bowls and place a slice of the baked bread in each one. Wash the chives, chop them finely and sprinkle on top.

Four servings

15 minutes

1 large white loaf (at least a day old)
125 ml (1/2 cup) milk
4 eggs
salt
pepper
4 tablespoons grated parmesan
1 litre (4 1/2 cups) meat stock (broth)
1 bunch chives
fat for baking sheet

Avocado Cream Soup

Four servings
20 minutes

2 ripe avocados
juice of 1 lemon
750 ml (3 1/2 cups)
vegetable stock (broth)
125 ml (1/2 cup) dry white
wine
salt
freshly ground white pepper
125 g / 4 1/2 oz (1/2 cup)
crème fraîche

1. Halve the avocados, remove the stone, peel and cut the flesh into chunks. Sprinkle immediately with lemon juice to stop them turning brown.

2. Mash the pieces of avocado with a fork and purée them. Put in a saucepan and gradually add the vegetable stock and white wine, stirring in well. Only add enough liquid to give the soup a creamy consistency.

3. Season the avocado cream with salt and pepper and add the crème fraîche. Bring briefly to the boil. Ladle into soup bowls and serve with croutons as desired.

Rocambole Garlic Soup

1. Wash the rocambole, pick it over and dry it. Cut into fine strips. Set some aside as a garnish for the soup and cook the rest in 250 ml/8 fl oz (1 cup) chicken stock for 5 minutes. Strain through a sieve and return the cooking liquid to the rest of the stock.

2. Peel the onions, dice finely and sweat in the heated butter. Add the cooked strips of rocambole and sauté briefly.

3. Add the rest of the stock. Beat the cornflour to a smooth paste with some cold water and stir it into the stock. Simmer for five minutes.

4. Stir in the crème fraîche. Season with salt and pepper.

5. Garnish with the reserved strips of rocambole and serve.

Four servings

20 minutes

120 g (4 oz) rocambole
garlic leaves
750 ml (3 1/2 cups) chicken
stock (broth)
2 small onions
2 tablespoons butter
2 tablespoons cornflour
(corn starch)
100 g / 3 1/2 oz (1/2 cup)
crème fraîche
salt
freshly ground black pepper

Beer Soup

Four servings

20 minutes

500 ml (2 1/4 cups) milk
50 g (1/4 cup) sugar
juice and zest of
1 unsprayed lemon
2 tablespoons cornflour
(corn starch)
1 egg white
1/2 teaspoon cinnamon
nutmeg
500 ml (2 1/4 cups) dark
beer
2 egg whites
1 tablespoon vanilla sugar

1. Bring the milk, sugar, lemon juice and lemon zest to the boil in a large saucepan.
2. Mix the cornflour with the egg yolk, add to the boiling milk and stir it in, beating constantly. Allow to boil briefly.
3. Add the cinnamon, some grated nutmeg and the beer. Re-heat the soup over a gentle heat but do not boil again.
4. Beat the egg whites with the vanilla sugar until they are stiff. Ladle the soup into soup plates, scoop up spoonfuls of the egg white mixture and slide them into the soup. Sprinkle cinnamon on top to taste.

Beer Soup

1. Place the mild and cinnamon stick in a pot and bring to the boil. In the meantime mix the cornflour in a little cold water and add to the boiling milk

2. Add the beer and reheat the soup.

3. Bind with egg yolk, and season the soup with sugar and salt to taste

Variation: Instead of a light beer, a malt beer may also be used.

Both variations may be seasoned with a small glass of brandy.

Four servings
20 minutes

500 ml (2 1/4 cups) milk
1 cinnamon stick
2 tablespoons cornflour
(corn starch)
2 bottles of light beer
1 egg yolk
sugar
salt

Bread Soup

Four servings
20 minutes

2 onions
3 tablespoons butter
4 slices stale black bread
100 g (1 cup) finely grated
Emmental cheese
1 litre (4 1/2 cups) meat
stock (broth)
freshly ground white pepper
1/2 bunch chives
salt

1. Peel the onions and cut into fine rings. Melt the butter in a pan and fry the onions slowly until a golden brown.
2. Arrange the onion rings on the bread slices and sprinkle with the grated cheese. Put in the oven for 5 minutes at 180 °C (350 °F), Gas mark 4, to melt the cheese. Bring the meat stock to the boil.
3. Lay the bread with the melted cheese in soup plates. Pour in the soup slowly from the edge so that the slices are barely covered and soak up the stock slowly from underneath.
4. Wash the chives and chop into little rings. Sprinkle them over the soup with the freshly ground pepper. Add salt to taste.

Fine Wine Soup

1. Heat butter in a pot. Add flour and let it brown while stirring constantly.

2. Add the water carefully while continuing to stir. Then add 50 g (3 1/2 tablespoons) sugar as well as the grated lemon rind. Let it cook for 10 minutes.

3. In the meantime mix the wine and egg yolk with a whisk and pour into the other ingredients in the pot.

4. Season the soup with the rest of the sugar and lemon juice.

Four servings
20 minutes

1 1/2 tablespoons butter
30 g (1/4 cup) wheat flour
1/2 l (2 cups) water
75 g (5 tablespoons) sugar
grated lemon rind
1/2 l (2 cups) white wine
1 egg yolk
juice from 1/2 lemon

91 Semolina Soup

Two to four servings
20 minutes

50 g (3 1/2 tablespoons) butter
60 g (1/2 cup) semolina
1 l (4 cups) beef or vegetable stock
nutmeg
rose paprika, fresh parsley

1. Melt the butter in a pot. Add the semolina and let it brown in the butter. Pour in the stock and bring to the boil. Simmer for 15 minutes over low heat.

2. Season the soup with the spices as desired. Sprinkle with freshly chopped parsley before serving.

92

Chilled Apple and Redcurrant Soup

Four servings
20 minutes

75 g (1 cup) rolled oats
250 ml (1 cup) milk
600 g (1 1/4 lb) untreated apples
juice of 1 lemon
60 ml (6 tablespoons) red-currant syrup or honey

1. Stir the oats into the milk and leave to swell for 20 minutes.
2. Wash the apples well, remove the cores and quarter. Grate finely.
3. Add the lemon juice and the syrup or honey to the apple. Mix well.
4. Stir the apple into the rolled oats. Refrigerate before serving.

1. Heat the stock in a pot and bring to the boil.

2. In the meantime mix the cheese with the butter and stir until creamy. Grate the apple and mix into the cheese-butter mixture together with the flour.

3. Stir the milk and mixture into the stock. Season with salt and caraway and let the soup simmer a while.

4. Remove the pot from the stove and beat in the eggs.

Two servings

10 minutes

3/4 l (3 cups) beef or vegetable stock
2 pieces of soft processed cheese
30 g (2 tablespoons) butter
1 large apple
40 g (1/3 cup) flour
1/4 l (1 cup) milk
salt
1/2 teaspoon ground caraway seeds
2 eggs

Coconut and Carrot Soup

One serving

20 minutes

1 spring onion (scallion)
1 teaspoon sunflower oil
3 large carrots
1 teaspoon lemon juice
125 ml (1/2 cup) vegetable
stock (broth)
50 ml (3 tablespoons)
coconut milk
1 pinch curry powder
salt
cayenne pepper
some fresh coriander leaves

1. Wash and prepare the spring onions and chop them finely. Heat the sunflower oil in a saucepan and fry the spring onions lightly. Wash and prepare the carrots, peel and cut into slices. Add the carrots to the onions and fry for a few minutes, stirring constantly.

2. Sprinkle lemon juice over the carrots, add the vegetable stock and simmer for about 15 minutes. Purée the vegetables in a blender, add the coconut milk and heat the soup again briefly. If the soup is too thick, add a little more vegetable stock.

3. Season the soup with curry powder, salt and cayenne pepper. Wash the coriander, chop the leaves coarsely and sprinkle over the soup.

1. Wash the herbs, dry them with a tea towel and remove the stalks. Chop finely on a large board and sprinkle with lemon juice.

2. Clean the spring onions and cut into fine rings. Heat the butter in a saucepan and sauté the onions. Dust with cornflour and add the chicken stock, stirring carefully to avoid lumps.

3. Add the white wine and cream and simmer for a few minutes. Add the chopped herbs and leave to steep for 5 minutes, but be careful not to boil it again.

4. Season the soup with salt, pepper and grated nutmeg and serve with croutons.

Four servings
20 minutes

Total of 150 g (6 oz) fresh herbs (for instance, chervil, tarragon, parsley, chives, sorrel, dill, watercress or lemon balm)
1 tablespoon lemon juice
3 spring onions (scallions)
1 tablespoon butter
1 tablespoon cornflour (corn starch)
500 ml (2 1/4 cups) chicken stock (broth)
125 ml (1/2 cup) white wine
125 ml / 4 fl oz (1/2 cup) cream
salt
pepper
nutmeg

Mediterranean Tomato Soup with Green Peppers

Four servings

20 minutes

4 shallots
2 unpeeled garlic cloves
8 tablespoons of olive oil
4 green peppers, washed
and sliced in rings
500 g (1 generous pound)
tomatoes, cut into quarters
750 ml / 25 fl oz (3 cups)
chicken stock
salt
pepper
2 teaspoon oregano
1/2 teaspoon rosemary

1. Mince the shallots; peel and mince 1 garlic clove. Heat the 4 tablespoons of the olive oil in a large pot. Stir in the shallots, chopped garlic and the whole garlic clove and allow them to simmer until the shallots become tender.
2. Add the green peppers and tomatoes and simmer for 2–3 minutes while continuing to stir. Add the chicken stock and bring to the boil. Let simmer for 5 minutes.
3. Season to taste with salt, pepper and herbs and let the soup stand for 2–3 minutes. Remove the whole garlic clove if desired.
4. Ladle the soup into four bowls and add a tablespoon of olive oil to each one before serving.

1. Mince the onion, garlic, ginger and lemon peel. Place in a pot and stir in the lemon juice and tomatoes. Bring to a boil and simmer for 5 minutes.

2. Add the fish stock, the fish and shrimps. Bring to a boil and simmer for 2–3 minutes. Season according to taste with soy sauce, salt and pepper.

Four servings

20 minutes

1 onion
3 cloves garlic
3 cm (1 1/4 inch) fresh ginger
juice and rind of 1 lemon
800 g (1 3/4 pound) tinned tomatoes
1 1/2 l / 51 fl oz (6 cups) fish stock
750 g (generous 1 1/2 pounds) codfish fillets cut into thick slices
250 g / generous 8 oz (2 3/4 cups) shrimps
1 tablespoon soy sauce
salt
pepper

Mussel Soup with Ginger

Four servings
20 minutes

4 stems lemongrass
2 cm (1 in) fresh ginger, peeled
3 garlic cloves, sliced
2 Chilies cut into rings
2 tablespoons sunflower oil
750 ml (3 cups) fish stock
250 g / 8 fl oz (1 cup) cream
Juice of 1/2 lemon
250 ml (1 cup) water
3 kg mussels
coconut stock

1. Finely chop as small as possible the lemon grass, ginger, garlic and chili. Heat oil in a pan, add the chopped ingredients and fry on a high heat. Add the fish stock and cream, bring to the boil and then simmer for 5–10 minutes.
2. In the meantime, bring the lemon juice and water to the boil in a deep pan. Add the mussels, and boil until then open. Divide between 4 large bowls.
3. Pour the coconut stock over the mussels and serve.

Plum Soup

1. Wash and stone the plums. Heat 1 litre / (4 1/2 cups) water in a large saucepan with a pinch of salt and cook the plums until soft.
2. Mix the cornflour with 1 tablespoon of cold water and beat slowly into the plums. Bring briefly to the boil and reduce the heat.
3. Add the cinnamon and sugar to the plums to taste and stir in the yoghurt. Ladle the plum soup into bowls and garnish with small macaroons or pieces of sweet biscuits.

Four servings
20 minutes

500 g (1 lb) plums
1 pinch of salt
1 tablespoon cornflour (corn starch)
1 teaspoon cinnamon
1 to 2 tablespoons icing (confectioner's) sugar
125 ml / 4 fl oz (1/2 cup) yoghurt

100 Gooseberry Soup

Four servings

20 minutes

500 g / 1 lb (2 cups) gooseberries
150 g / 5 oz (2/3 cup) sugar
250 ml / 8 fl oz (1 cup) white
wine
250 ml / 8 fl oz (1 cup) unfilt-
ered apple juice
1 pinch curry powder
4 sprigs lemon balm

1. Wash the gooseberries, remove the stalks and the little hairs.
2. Put the sugar in a heavy pan and allow to caramelize until it is light brown. Add the gooseberries and pour the wine and apple juice over them. Stir in the curry powder and simmer covered for 10 minutes.
3. Wash the lemon balm, chop the leaves from two of the sprigs and add to the soup. Blend the soup and pass through a sieve.
4. Serve garnished with the remaining leaves of lemon balm.

1. Cut the tomatoes criss-cross at the stem and place into a bowl. Pour boiling water over them. Set in a sieve over a large pot and remove the skins.

2. Puree the tomatoes in a blender together with some of the stock. Add the rest of the stock and seasonings. Pour the mixture into the pot and heat without boiling.

3. Add 1 tablespoon of lemon juice and pour the soup into pre-warmed bowls. Garnish with a tablespoon of basil, grated lemon rind and black pepper before serving.

Four servings
20 minutes

1 kg (scant 4 1/2 pounds) ripe tomatoes
500 ml (2 cups) chicken stock
juice and grated rind of 1 lemon
salt
pepper
bunch of basil, cut finely

102 Mushroom Cream Soup

Four servings

25 minutes

3 spring onions (scallions)
2 tablespoons butter
250 g / 8 oz (2 cups) fresh
mushrooms
3 tablespoons plain (all purpose) flour
125 ml / 4 fl oz (1/2 cup) milk
500 ml / 16 fl oz (2 1/4 cups)
vegetable stock (broth)
125 ml / 4 fl oz (1/2 cup)
white wine
125 ml / 4 fl oz (1/2 cup)
cream
salt
freshly ground white pepper
nutmeg
1 bunch parsley
croutons

1. Clean the spring onions and cut into fine rings. Melt the butter in a large pan and sweat the onions.

2. Rub the mushrooms with a tea towel, cut into fine slices and sweat them briefly. Dust with flour and stir. After about 2 minutes, pour in the milk and stir carefully to avoid lumps.

3. Add the vegetable stock and white wine. Simmer for 15 minutes. Purée the soup. Add the cream, bring briefly to the boil again, remove from the heat and add salt, pepper and grated nutmeg to taste.

4. Wash the parsley and chop finely. Ladle the soup into soup bowls, sprinkle with parsley and serve with croutons.

Mushroom Cream Soup II

1. Pour stock into a pot and bring to the boil.
2. In the meantime clean the champignons and chop finely in the food processor.
3. Melt the butter in a pot and add the champignons. Allow them to simmer over low heat for 10 minutes. Then sprinkle the flour over the champignons. Add the boiling stock little by little while stirring continuously.
4. Stir in the heavy cream and bring mixture quickly to the boil once more. Season the soup with spices and sprinkle with chopped parsley before serving.

Two to four servngs
25 minutes

1 l (4 cups) boiling beef or vegetable stock
200 g / 7 oz (1 3/4 cups) fresh champignons
3 tablespoons butter
1 heaping tablespoon flour
250 g / 9 oz (1 cup) heavy cream
salt
pepper
rose paprika
freshly chopped parsley

104 Egg Strips

Four servings

25 minutes

For 1 litre (4 1/2 cups) of
soup:
2 eggs
4 tablespoons milk
1 tablespoon cream
salt
pepper
nutmeg
1 teaspoon butter

1. Beat the eggs with the milk and cream in a bowl.

2. Season with salt, pepper and a little grated nutmeg. Put the egg mixture in a buttered jelly mould with a smooth base. Place the mould in a bain marie and steam for about 15 minutes until the egg mixture sets.

3. Remove the mould from water, leave to cool and ease the egg mixture out onto a flat plate. Cut it into thin strips, cubes or diamond shapes, or cut out other shapes with pastry cutters. Place in the soup plates and add hot soup.

1. Peel and quarter the tomatoes and remove the seeds. Peel the onions and garlic. Peel the cucumber and cut in half lengthways; remove the seeds and dice. Cut the red pepper in half, remove the seeds and cut into eight pieces.

2. Cut one-third of the tomatoes, onions, garlic, cucumber and red pepper into small cubes. Purée the rest in the blender with oil and vinegar and season with salt and pepper. Pour the gazpacho in a bowl, cover and chill in the refrigerator.

3. Just before serving, cut slices of white bread into small cubes. Heat some butter in a pan and fry the bread cubes until golden brown. Put in a small bowl as with the other diced vegetables and serve with the soup.

Two servings
25 minutes

800 g (1 3/4 lb) ripe tomatoes
2 onions
2–3 cloves garlic
1 cucumber
1 green pepper
1 red pepper
3 tablespoons olive oil
1 tablespoon wine vinegar
salt
freshly ground pepper
2–3 slices white bread, crusts removed
25 g (2 tablespoons) butter

106 Oat Flour Soup

Four servings

25 minutes

2 tablespoons butter
60 g (1/2 cup) finely ground
oat flour
500 ml (2 1/4 cups) milk
1 pinch salt
1 tablespoon vanilla sugar
50 g (scant 1/2 cup) icing
(confectioner's) sugar
50 g (3/8 cup) almonds
50 g (1/3 cup) dried fruit
such as prunes and apricots

1. Melt the butter in a large saucepan. Add the oat flour and brown while stirring constantly.
2. Add the milk and 500 ml/17 fl oz (2 1/4 cups) water to the roux and beat briskly. Cook over a medium heat for 10 to 15 minutes.
3. Add the salt, vanilla sugar and icing sugar to the oat soup to taste. Finely chop the almonds and stir into the soup. Add the dried fruit and cook gently in the simmering soup for another couple of minutes.

1. Heat the butter and oil in a pot. Add the shallots and leeks and simmer until they are tender.

2. In the meantime cut the potatoes into thin slices; stir them into the leeks together with the stock and salt. Bring to a boil and simmer at low heat for 15 minutes. Add the heavy cream and then pour into the food processor. Blend until smooth. Season as desired with salt. Sprinkle with finely chopped chives before serving.

Four servings

25 minutes

1 tablespoon butter
1 tablespoon sunflower oil
3 shallots sliced into thin rings
3 leeks sliced into thin rings
2 large potatoes
250 ml (1 cup) vegetable stock
salt
150 g / 5 oz (scant 2/3 cup) heavy cream
chives

Potato Soup

Two servings

25 minutes

3 large floury potatoes
2 carrots
1 parsley root
2 sticks (stalks) celery
750 ml (3 1/2 cups)
vegetable stock (broth)
250 ml (1 cup) low-fat milk
(1.5 %)
freshly ground pepper
salt
some dried marjoram
200 g (7 oz) low-fat sea fish
(for instance rosefish)
some sprigs of parsley

1. Peel the potatoes, carrots and parsley root. Cut the potatoes into thin slices. Cut the carrots and parsley root into large cubes. Wash the celery and chop coarsely.
2. Heat the vegetable stock and milk in a large saucepan and add the vegetables. Cook for about 10–15 minutes until tender.
3. Purée the vegetable soup with a hand-mixer and season with salt, pepper and marjoram.
4. Cut the fish into thin strips and add to the soup. Cook over a low heat for about 5 minutes. Wash the parsley, dab dry, chop the leaves and sprinkle over the soup.

Spicy Creamed Pumpkin and Mustard Soup

1. Peel the pumpkin, remove the seeds and finely dice the flesh. Peel the potatoes and cut into cubes. Peel the onion and garlic and chop finely.

2. Heat the oil in a saucepan and fry the onion until transparent. Add the garlic and fry briefly with the onion. Add the diced pumpkin and potato and continue frying. Pour in the stock, cover and simmer the vegetables for about 15 minutes.

3. Take two tablespoons of diced pumpkin and put to one side. Add the cream and crème fraîche to the soup and purée with a hand-mixer. Season with mustard, salt and white pepper.

4. Pour the soup into two bowls, garnish with the diced pumpkin and sprinkle pumpkin seed oil over it.

Two servings

25 minutes

1 piece pumpkin (about 200 g; 7 oz)
1 potato (50 g; 2 oz)
1 onion
1 clove garlic
1 teaspoon sunflower oil
250 ml (1 cup) vegetable stock (broth)
75 ml / 8 fl oz (3/8 cup) cream
1 tablespoon crème fraîche
3 teaspoons medium strength mustard
sea salt
freshly ground white pepper
2 teaspoons pumpkin seed oil

110

Brussels Sprouts and Leek Soup

Two servings

25 minutes

250 g (9 oz) Brussels sprouts
2 leeks
1 stick (stalk) celery
1 onion
1 teaspoon olive oil
400 ml (1 3/4 cups) vegetable stock (broth)
sea salt
freshly grated nutmeg
freshly ground pepper
1 bunch basil
1 tablespoon grated Parmesan

1. Wash and prepare the Brussels sprouts and cut them into half. Wash and prepare the leeks and celery and cut them into fine strips. Peel the onions and chop finely.

2. Heat the olive oil in a large saucepan and fry the onion until transparent. Add the vegetables and fry them briefly. Pour in the stock, cover and simmer the vegetables for about 20 minutes over a low heat.

3. Season the soup with salt, grated nutmeg and freshly ground pepper. Wash the basil, cut the leaves into fine strips and sprinkle over the soup. Pour the soup in two bowls and sprinkle with Parmesan.

1. Cut the stale bread into large cubes of about 2 cm / 1 in. Peel and chop the onion finely. Cut the bacon into small pieces. Melt the butter in a large saucepan and, fry the onions and bacon until golden brown.

2. Add the bread and fry briefly. Put the contents of the pan in a bowl and allow to cool. Meanwhile beat the egg with the cream and season with salt and pepper. Pour the egg mixture over the bread cubes and allow them to soak it up.

3. Add the flour and parsley and knead the mixture well by hand. If the consistency seems too soft, add some breadcrumbs.

4. Heat the stock. With cool, moist hands form the dough into dumplings with a diameter of about 7 cm / 3 in and lower them carefullly into the stock. Simmer gently for about 10 minutes until they rise to the surface.

Four servings
25 minutes

4 thick slices of white bread (at least a day old)
2 onions
50 g (2 oz) smoked bacon
1/2 tablespoon butter
1 egg
125 ml / 4 fl oz (1/2 cup) cream
salt
pepper
1 tablespoon flour
2 tablespoons chopped parsley
breadcrumbs
1.5 litres (7 cups) meat stock (broth)

Sweet Potato Soup

Four servings
25 minutes

1 onion
2 cloves garlic pressed
1/2 teaspoon dried ginger
1/4 teaspoon chili flakes
3 tablespoons sunflower oil
juice of 1 lemon
2 large sweet potatoes, cut into pieces
1 l (4 cups) chicken stock
150 g / 5 oz (scant 2/3 cup) heavy cream
salt, pepper

1. Chop the onion, garlic, ginger and chili as fine as possible and brown in a pot together with the oil and lemon juice for 3–5 minutes.
2. Add the sweet potatoes and brown for 2–3 minutes while stirring constantly. Then pour in the stock and heavy cream and simmer until the potatoes are tender.
3. Pour the soup into the food processor and blend until smooth. Season and serve immediately.

113

Onion Soup

1. Heat the butter in a pot. Chop the onions finely and simmer in the butter.
2. Lower the heat and sprinkle the flour on the onions. Add the crème fraîche while stirring continuously.
3. Add the stock a little at a time, continuing to stir all the while. Then season the soup well and serve.

Two to four servings
25 minutes

1 tablespoon butter
250 g (1/2 pound) onions
3–4 tablespoons flour
50 g (1/4 cup) crème fraîche
1 1/4 l (5 cups) vegetable broth
salt, pepper

1. Cook the pudding rice following the instructions on the packet.

2. Wash the apples thoroughly. Do not peel or core, but cut into large chunks. Bring 1 litre (4 1/2 cups) water to the boil in a saucepan and cook the apples and lemon peel until soft.

3. Pass the cooked apples through a sieve to obtain a fine consistency. Add sugar to taste.

4. Heat the custard, add eggnog and fold into the apple sauce.

5. Spoon 2 to 3 tablespoons of rice pudding onto each plate and pour the apple sauce over it.

Four servings

30 minutes

80 g (3/8 cup) pudding rice
650 g (1 1/2 lb) untreated apples
peel from 1 unsprayed lemon
sugar
250 ml (1 cup) custard
4 tablespoons eggnog

115 Artichoke Soup

Four servings

30 minutes

10 artichoke hearts
2 onions
40 g (3 tablespoons) butter
juice of 1/2 lemon
1 litre (4 1/2 cups) vegetable
stock (broth)
salt
pepper
250 ml / 8 fl oz (1 cup) cream
4 artichoke hearts for
garnish
50 g (3/8 cup) shrimps
grated parmesan

1. Wash the artichoke hearts and cut off the hard tops. Peel and quarter the onions. Melt the butter in a large saucepan and sweat the onions.

2. Add 10 of the artichoke hearts, sprinkle with lemon juice and cook for 5 minutes. Add the vegetable stock and simmer the soup for 20 minutes. Remove the pan from heat, purée the soup and pass it through a fine sieve.

3. Season with salt and pepper to taste. Add the cream and bring briefly to the boil again.

4. Arrange shrimps on the 4 reserved artichokes, sprinkle with parmesan and brown quickly under the grill. Ladle the soup into soup plates and garnish each with a shrimp "boat".

1. Open the oysters with an oyster knife, remove them from their shells and sprinkle with lemon juice. Heat fish stock and white wine together, add the oysters and cook gently for several minutes.

2. Remove the oysters from the stock and arrange in four soup bowls. Heat the olive oil in a large saucepan, dust with cornflour, stir and brown over a low heat. Pour on the fish stock stirring constantly and simmer for 15 minutes.

3. Add salt, pepper and sherry to taste. Keep the soup warm on a low heat and stir in the crème fraîche. Wash the parsley and chop finely. Pour the hot soup over the oysters, sprinkle with parsley and serve with a fresh baguette.

Four servings
30 minutes

16 fresh oysters
2 tablespoons lemon juice
750 ml (3 1/2 cups) fish stock (broth)
250 ml (1 cup) white wine
3 tablespoons olive oil
2 tablespoons cornflour (corn starch)
salt
pepper
1 tablespoon sherry
125 g / 4 oz (5/8 cup) crème fraîche
1 bunch parsley

Brown Roux Soup

Four servings
30 minutes

50 g (1/4 cup) butter
70 g (3/4 cup) white flour
1 litre (4 1/2 cups) meat
stock (broth)

1. Melt the butter in a pan and allow to become light brown. Add the flour and beat until smooth. Sweat gently over medium heat until brown.

2. Gradually add the liquid, beating to keep it smooth.

3. Simmer the soup for about 20 minutes so that the flour loses its uncooked taste.

1. Peel and finely chop the shallots and spring onions. Melt butter in a large casserole dish and fry the onions until lightly golden.

2. Mix in the tomato purée and season with a little chilli and salt. Add 250 ml/8 fl oz (1 cup) of the stock and simmer for 10 minutes.

3. Remove the soup from heat and liquidize. Add the rest of the stock and heat again gently. Gradually add the peanut butter to the hot soup with a spoon and then beat thoroughly.

4. Finally add the coconut milk and let the soup simmer gently for a few minutes. Season with salt, freshly ground pepper and lemon juice.

Four servings

30 minutes

3 shallots
3 spring onions (scallions)
1 tablespoon butter
1 tablespoon tomato purée
chilli powder
salt
750 ml (3 1/2 cups) veg-
etable stock (broth)
5 tablespoons peanut butter
3 tablespoons coconut milk
freshly ground white pepper
1 tablespoon lemon juice

Green Asparagus Soup

Four servings

30 minutes

1 kg (2 lb) fresh green
asparagus
salt
1 teaspoon sugar
1 teaspoon butter
2 tablespoons cornflour
(corn starch)
200 ml / 7 fl oz (7/8 cup)
cream
freshly ground white pepper
zest and juice of
1 untreated lemon
1 bunch parsley

1. Wash the green asparagus and cut off the stringy ends. Peel only the bottom half and cut the whole into pieces.

2. In a large saucepan, bring 1 litre (4 1/2 cups) salt water to the boil with the sugar and the butter. Add the asparagus and simmer gently for 15 to 20 minutes.

3. Remove the pan from heat and purée the soup. Mix the cornflour with some cream and stir into the soup with a balloon whisk. Briefly bring to the boil again.

4. Add the rest of the cream and season the soup with salt, pepper and the zest and juice of the lemon. Wash the parsley, chop the leaves finely and sprinkle over the soup.

1. Heat the butter until it sizzles but do not let it become brown. Add the flour and beat until smooth. Cook over gentle heat.

2. Add the liquid gradually, beating to keep it smooth.

3. Simmer the soup for about 20 minutes so that the taste of uncooked flour is no longer present.

Four servings

30 minutes

50 g (1/4 cup) butter
50 g (1/2 cup) white flour
1 litre (4 1/2 cups) meat, fish or vegetable stock (broth)

Potato and Buttermilk Soup

Four servings

30 minutes

1 litre (4 1/2 cups) buttermilk
2 tablespoons plain (all purpose) flour
250 g (8 oz) floury potatoes
salt
pepper
2 spring onions (scallions)
1 tablespoon butter
200 g (7 oz) cooked ham
several sprigs chervil

1. Pour the buttermilk into a saucepan, stir in the flour with a balloon whisk and bring to the boil.

2. Peel the potatoes and cut into small pieces. Simmer in the buttermilk for 20 minutes until they are soft. Add salt and pepper to taste.

3. Wash and prepare the spring onions, cut into fine rings. Heat butter in a pan and cook the onions over a low heat. Finely dice the ham and add to the pan, browning for several minutes.

4. Wash the chervil and chop fine. Ladle the soup into soup plates, add the fried ham and onions and sprinkle chervil on top.

1. Scrub the mussels thoroughly, remove the hairy beards and rinse several times. Discard any open or damaged specimens. Peel shallots and garlic. Dice shallots and crush garlic.

2. Heat two tablespoons of oil in a saucepan and sauté the shallots and garlic until they become transparent. Add wine, thyme and mussels. Add a cup of water and simmer for 10 minutes in a saucepan with the lid on until the mussels open.

3. Remove the mussels from their shells. Save the liquor, strain it through a fine sieve, cover and set aside.

4. Peel the carrots and potatoes and dice very finely. Heat the rest of the oil and sweat the vegetables in it. Add the cooking liquor from the mussels and the chicken stock and cook for about 10 minutes. Add the lemon juice, salt and pepper to taste. Return the mussels to the soup and reheat.

5. Remove soup from heat, mix crème fraîche and egg yolks together and thicken the soup with the mixture. Serve sprinkled with parsley.

Four servings

30 minutes

1 kg (2 lb) mussels
4 shallots
2 cloves garlic
4 tablespoons olive oil
125 ml (1/2 cup) dry white wine
2 sprigs thyme
2 carrots
2 potatoes
750 ml (3 1/2 cups) chicken stock (broth)
juice of 1 lemon
salt
freshly ground white pepper
100 g / 3 1/2 oz (1/2 cup) crème fraîche
2 egg yolks
2 tablespoons chopped parsley

123 Milk Soup

Four servings

30 minutes

70 g (3/4 cup) rye flour
50 g (1/2 cup) grated
Emmental cheese
500 ml (2 1/4 cups) milk
500 ml (2 1/4 cups) buttermilk
salt
freshly ground white pepper
nutmeg

1. Knead the rye flour with the grated cheese and 3 to 4 tablespoons water into a firm dough. If the dough is too crumbly, add a little more water.

2. Refrigerate the dough for 15 minutes, then roll it out on a wooden board and cut into short noodles with a knife.

3. Bring the milk, buttermilk and salt to the boil, add the noodles and leave to steep over low heat for 5 minutes until they are done. Add salt, pepper and grated nutmeg to the milk soup to taste.

1. Melt the butter in a large saucepan. Peel and chop the shallots, then sweat in the butter until transparent.

2. Peel and dice the carrots and potatoes, add to the shallots and sweat them too. Add the vegetable stock and the milk and simmer for 20 minutes on a gentle heat with the lid on.

3. Remove the soup from the heat, purée it and stir in the crème fraîche. If the soup is too thick, add a little more milk and bring to the boil again. Add salt, pepper, some grated nutmeg and the orange juice to taste.

4. Wash the parsley, remove the stalks and chop it finely. Ladle the soup into soup plates, sprinkle over the parsley and serve with the croutons.

Two servings
10 minutes

2 tablespoons butter
2 shallots
500 g (1 lb) carrots
200 g (7 oz) floury potatoes
750 ml (3 1/2 cups) veg-
etable stock (broth)
250 ml (1 cup) milk
125 g / 4 oz (5/8 cup) crème
fraîche
salt
freshly ground white pepper
nutmeg
juice of 1 orange
1 bunch flat-leaf parsley
croutons

Spicy Tomato Soup with Avocado and Shrimps

Six servings

30 minutes

1 red onion
2 large tins tomatoes
(800 g / 1 3/4 lb each)
5 tablespoons olive oil
2 cloves garlic
1/2 teaspoon oregano
1/2 teaspoon chilli powder
salt
1 teaspoon powdered
vegetable stock (broth)
1 tablespoon sugar
4 slices white bread
1 avocado
juice of 1 lemon
1 yellow pepper
2 tablespoons chopped
parsley
a few dashes of Tabasco
100 g (3 1/2 oz) shrimps
1 tablespoon chopped basil

1. Chop the onions coarsely. Strain the tomatoes through a sieve and reserve the juice.

2. Heat 2 tablespoons oil in a large saucepan. Add the diced onion, 1 pressed clove of garlic, and fry lightly. Add the strained tomatoes and juice and stir. Add the vegetable stock and season with oregano, chilli powder, salt and sugar; simmer for about 10 minutes. Taste and season again if necessary.

3. Remove the crusts from the slices of white bread and cut into small cubes. Heat the remaining oil in a pan and fry the diced bread; add 1 pressed garlic clove and put to one side.

4. Halve the avocado lengthways, remove the stone and take out the flesh with a spoon. Dice the avocado flesh, put in a bowl and sprinkle immediately with half the lemon juice.

5. Wash the yellow pepper, dice and add to the diced avocado. Add the chopped parsley and mix well. Season generously with salt and tabasco.

6. Place the shrimps into a bowl and stir in the chopped basil and the remaining lemon juice. Serve the croutons and avocado mixture separately in bowls to accompany the soup.

1. Wash the rhubarb, peel and cut into 2 cm / 1 in pieces. Heat 1 litre (4 1/2 cups) water in a large saucepan and add the rhubarb, sugar, raspberry syrup, lemon zest and lemon juice.
2. Cook over a gentle heat until the rhubarb is soft. Mix the cornflour with 2 tablespoons of cold water and beat into the hot soup. Bring briefly to the boil until the soup thickens.
3. Serve in shallow bowls with the rusks. Chop the hazelnuts coarsely and sprinkle on top of the soup.

Four servings

30 minutes

500 g (1 lb) rhubarb
120 g (generous 1/2 cup) sugar
3 tablespoons raspberry syrup
zest and juice of 1/2 untreated lemon
2 tablespoons cornflour (corn starch)
50 g (1/2 cup) hazelnuts (filberts)
rusks (zwieback crackers)

127 Spinach Cream Soup

Four servings

30 minutes

1 tablespoon butter
2 shallots
300 g (10 oz) fresh spinach
750 ml (3 1/2 cups)
vegetable stock (broth)
1 large floury potato
nutmeg
salt
freshly ground white pepper
100 g / 3 1/2 oz (1/2 cup)
crème fraîche
50 g (3/8 cup) pine kernels

1. Heat the butter in a large saucepan. Peel and chop the shallots, then sweat in the butter until transparent. Wash the spinach and add to the shallots. Steam until the spinach collapses slightly.

2. Add the vegetable stock. Peel the potato and finely dice. Add to the soup and simmer for 10 to 15 minutes with the lid on, until the potatoes are done.

3. Purée the soup and season with grated nutmeg, salt and pepper. Over a very low heat, fold in the crème fraîche. Do not let the soup boil again.

4. Ladle the soup into bowls, and sprinkle with chopped pine kernels. Serve with fresh white bread.

Creamed Tomato Soup with Wine

1. Cut the ham into small cubes. Heat the oil in a large pan and fry the diced ham briefly.
2. Pour the tomatoes though a sieve and reserve the liquid. Dice the tomatoes. Put the diced tomatoes and juice into a saucepan and stir. Add the beef stock and wine. Bring the soup to the boil and simmer for about 15 minutes.
3. Put the curd cheese, crème fraîche and tomato purée in a bowl and stir until the mixture is smooth. Add 2 cups of stock to this mixture and stir well. Stir the crème fraîche into the soup and bring back to the boil. Season the tomato soup to taste with salt and pepper.

Four servings
30 minutes

200 g (7 oz) cooked ham
2 tablespoons oil
1 tin tomatoes (400 g; 14 oz)
500 ml (2 1/4 cups) beef stock (broth)
200 ml (7/8 cup) white wine
200 g (7 oz) curd cheese
100 g / 3 1/2 oz (1/2 cup) crème fraîche
2 tablespoons tomato purée
salt
pepper

Tomato and Bacon Soup

Four servings

30 minutes

4 small onions
1 kg (2 1/4 lb) tomatoes
1–2 cloves garlic
80 g (3 oz) streaky bacon
40 g (6 tablespoons) flour
750 ml (3 1/2 cups) beef stock (broth)
salt
freshly ground pepper
paprika pepper
chopped thyme
100 ml / 3 1/2 fl oz (1/2 cup) cream
a few leaves of basil as garnish

1. Peel the onions and chop finely. Peel the tomatoes, cut into quarters and remove the seeds. Peel and press the cloves of garlic

2. Finely dice the bacon stir and melt in a pan. Add the chopped onion and sweat until transparent. Sprinkle the flour on top and brown lightly. Add the tomato pieces to the pan and braise briefly. Pour the beef stock over all.

3. Season the soup with salt, pepper, paprika, thyme and garlic. Cover and simmer on a low heat for 15 minutes.

4. Beat the cream until semi-stiff. Strain the soup through a sieve and return to the pan. Reheat and season again. Pour into bowls and garnish with a spoonful of cream and basil leaves.

1. Melt the butter in a large saucepan, sprinkle in the cornflour and brown it lightly. Pour the white wine onto this roux and beat in carefully. Gradually add 500 ml (2 1/4 cups) water and bring slowly to the boil.

2. Add the sugar, vanilla sugar, lemon zest, cloves, cinnamon stick and cardamom to the saucepan and simmer everything for 20 minutes.

3. Strain the wine soup through a fine sieve to remove the spices. Beat the egg yolk in another large saucepan and gradually add the wine soup. Bring slowly to the boil over a gentle heat while stirring constantly to a creamy consistency. Ladle into small bowls and serve with butter biscuits.

Four servings
30 minutes

1 tablespoon butter
2 tablespoons cornflour
(corn starch)
1 litre (4 1/2 cups) fruity
white wine
150 g (3/4 cup) sugar
1 teaspoon vanilla sugar
zest from 1 untreated lemon
4 cloves
1 cinnamon stick
pinch of cardamom
6 egg yolks

131 Lemon Rice Soup

Four servings

30 minutes

1 litre (4 1/2 cups) vegetable
stock (broth)
juice of 2 lemons
2 stalks lemongrass
2 spring onions (scallions)
4 tablespoons basmati rice
1 teaspoon sugar
1 tablespoon dry sherry
salt
pepper
soy sauce
zest of 1 untreated lemon
1 whole untreated lemon
several mint leaves

1. Bring the vegetable stock and lemon juice to the boil in a large saucepan. Beat the lemongrass stalks to flatten them slightly and add to the stock. Clean the spring onions, cut into fine rings and add them.

2. Wash the rice and stir into the boiling soup. Reduce the heat and simmer for 20 minutes with the lid on. Remove the lemongrass stalks.

3. Add sugar, sherry, salt, pepper and a dash of soy sauce for a piquant flavour. Add the lemon zest and leave the soup to steep for another 3 to 4 minutes.

4. Wash the whole lemon and cut it into eight segments. Ladle the soup into Asian soup bowls and garnish with the lemon segments and the mint leaves.

1. For the dressing: mix the salad cream or mayonnaise, sour cream, lemon juice, vinegar, pepper, salt, sugar and dill in a bowl.

2. Cut the cheese into cubes of 1 cm (1/2 in).

3. Wash the apples thoroughly, remove the cores and quarter. Cut the quarters into fine slices. Carefully mix the cheese and apple slices together in a bowl.

4. Chop the walnuts and sprinkle over the apple and cheese mixture. Serve the dressing in a separate bowl.

Four servings

10 minutes

4 tablespoons salad cream or mayonnaise
125 ml / 4 fl oz (1/2 cup) sour cream
juice of 1/2 lemon
2 tablespoons vinegar
freshly ground black pepper
pinch of salt
sprinkling of sugar
1 tablespoon chopped dill
300 g (10 oz) hard cheese
400 g (14 oz) untreated red apples
100 g / 3 1/2 oz (1 cup) walnuts

133

Chicory and Apple Salad

Four servings
10 minutes

6 chicory heads
700 g (1 1/2 lb) untreated
apples
salt
sugar
1 tablespoon lemon juice
cream

1. Wash the chicory, cut in half and remove the core. Cut crossways into fine strips.
2. Peel the apples, remove the cores and quarter. Grate the apples finely.
3. Mix apples and chicory in a bowl, season with salt and sugar and sprinkle with lemon juice. Add cream to taste if desired.

134

Apple Salad Romantique

1. Peel the apples, remove the cores and quarter. Cut the quarters into cubes.
2. Put the apple cubes in a bowl and marinate with the sugar and the lemon juice.
3. Add the raisins to the apples and add sugar and lemon juice to taste.

Four servings
10 minutes

400 g (14 oz) untreated
apples
50 g / 2 oz (1/4 cup) sugar
juice of 1 lemon
150 g / 5 oz (3/4 cup) raisins

1. Drain the tuna in a sieve and break up with a fork.

2. Wash the apples thoroughly, remove the cores and quarter. Cut into cubes.

3. Peel the onion and cut into fine rings. Wash and dry the lettuce, then divide the leaves between the four plates. Arrange the apples, tuna and onions on the lettuce leaves.

4. For the sauce: put the yoghurt in a bowl and season with the lemon juice, sugar, salt and pepper. Pour over the salad and serve.

Four servings
10 minutes

2 tins of tuna in oil
400 g (14 oz) untreated apples
1 onion
1/2 head green lettuce
125 ml / 4 fl oz (1/2 cup) plain yoghurt
juice of 1 lemon
sprinkling of sugar
pinch of salt
freshly ground pepper

Bean Salad with Green Peppers

Four servings

10 minutes

2 green peppers, washed and cut in strips
2 tablespoons balsamic vinegar
2 tablespoons soy sauce
2 tablespoons medium-strength mustard
100 ml (generous 6 tablespoons) olive oil
750 g (generous 1 1/2 pounds) green beans (tinned)
salt
pepper
1 tablespoon savoury

1. Boil water in a pot and blanche the green peppers for 1/2 minute. Rinse the paprika slices briefly under cold running water.
2. Combine vinegar, soy sauce and mustard. While stirring steadily, add the oil until the mixture thickens.
3. Place the beans and paprika into a bowl and add the sauce. Mix well. Season with salt, pepper and savoury.

1. Heat oil and butter in a pan and then add the diced bread. Sauté until golden. After a minute add the garlic, but be careful not to let it burn. Place garlic and croutons on a paper towel to absorb excess oil. Set aside.

2. In a small shallow bowl, combine the olive oil and lemon juice and dredge the lettuce leaves in the mixture.

3. Divide the croutons onto four large salad bowls and place the lettuce leaves on top. Season with salt and pepper. Top with a few drops of Worchestershire sauce, chopped eggs and Parmesan before serving.

Two servings
10 minutes

2 large slices of white bread, diced
butter for sautéing
1 large garlic clove, finely chopped
3 tablespoons olive oil
1/2 tablespoon lemon juice
1 small lettuce head
salt
pepper
1 teaspoon Worcestershire sauce
2 hard-boiled eggs, freshly boiled, peeled and chopped
grated Parmesan cheese

138 Fruit Salad with Lemon Dressing

Two servings
10 minutes

1 banana
1 apricot
1 slice honeydew melon
(about 200 g; 7 oz)
1 clementine
1 tablespoon lemon juice
1 tablespoon maple syrup
1 tablespoon crème fraîche

1. Peel the banana and cut into slices, peel the apricot, halve it, remove the stone (pit) and cut into quarters. Peel the honeydew melon, remove the seeds and cut into small pieces. Peel the clementines and divide into segments. Arrange the fruit in two bowls.

2. Make the sauce with the lemon juice, maple syrup and crème fraîche and pour over the fruit.

139 Asparagus and Radicchio Salad with Parma Ham

1. Wash the asparagus, remove the woody ends and cut into pieces about 2.5 cm/1 in in length. Cook in salted boiling water for about 8 minutes until done.

2. Clean and wash the radicchio, cut into thin strips and stir into the asparagus.

3. Mix the cider vinegar, apple juice, pepper, salt and oil together to make a vinaigrette and pour over the salad. Sprinkle with Parmesan shavings and garnish with the Parma ham.

Four servings
10 minutes

400 g (14 oz) green
asparagus
salt
75 g (3 oz) Radicchio salad
3 tablespoons cider vinegar
3 tablespoons apple juice
freshly ground pepper
1 teaspoon oil
2 tablespoons Parmesan
cheese, shaved
4 slices Parma ham

1. Wash and prepare the salad and the vegetables. Cut the carrots and pepper into matchsticks and put in a small salad bowl together with the rocket.

2. Make a salad dressing with lemon juice, pepper, balsamic vinegar and olive oil. Wash the chives, chop and add to the dressing.

3. Spread some diet margarine on a slice of wholemeal rye bread and put a slice of Parma ham on top. Pour the dressing over the salad just before serving and mix carefully.

Two servings

10 minutes

1 bunch rocket (about 80 g; 3 oz)
1 small carrot
1/2 red sweet pepper
1 tablespoon lemon juice
freshly ground pepper
1 tablespoon balsamic vinegar
1 teaspoon olive oil
1/2 bunch chives
1 slice wholemeal rye bread
1 teaspoon diet margarine
2 thin slices Parma ham

Beetroot (Red Beet) Salad

Two servings

10 minutes

100 g (3 1/2 oz) steamed beetroot (red beet)
1 chicory head
1 orange
salt
freshly ground pepper
1 teaspoon balsamic vinegar
1/2 carton low-fat yoghurt (1.5%)
1 teaspoon chopped walnuts
1 slice wholemeal (whole-wheat) bread

1. Cut the beetroot (red beet) in half and then into slices. Divide the leaves of the chicory and arrange them decoratively in a soup plate.
2. Peel the orange and divide into segments. Arrange the beetroot (red beet) slices and orange segments on the chicory leaves. Mix salt, pepper, balsamic vinegar and yoghurt together to make a dressing.
3. Pour the dressing over the salad, sprinkle chopped walnuts on top and serve with a slice of wholemeal bread.

Sausage in Aspic (Sülzwurst) Salad

1. Dice the sausage aspic and the cucumber and grate the onion over them.

2. Combine vinegar, oil and salt in a small bowl. Dice the pickles and stir into the dressing together with the chives and parsley. Pour the dressing over the jellied sausage-cucumber salad and mix carefully.

3. Place the salad on the toasted bread and serve.

Two servings
10 minutes

350 g / 12 oz sausage in aspic (Sülzwurst)
1 small salad cucumber
1 onion
vinegar
oil
salt
2 pickles
fresh chives, finely chopped
fresh parsley, finely chopped
4 slices of bread, lightly toasted

Tomato Salad with Bananas

Four servings

10 minutes

2 ripe bananas
1 tablespoon lemon juice
500 g (18 oz) firm tomatoes
2 tablespoons balsamic
vinegar
6 tablespoons sunflower oil
1/2 teaspoon medium-
strength mustard
salt
pepper
curry powder
sugar
1 bunch flat leaf parsley

1. Peel and slice the bananas and sprinkle with lemon juice. Peel the tomatoes, cut in half and slice. Put the tomato and banana slices in a bowl and mix together carefully.

2. For the salad dressing: mix the vinegar, oil and mustard together and stir vigorously. Season to taste with salt, pepper, curry powder and sugar. Pour the dressing over the salad and stir gently.

3. Arrange the salad on four plates and sprinkle with chopped parsley.

Tomato Salad with Hidden Eggs

1. Butter the slices of bread. Peel the eggs and cut in half.

2. Combine the sour cream, tomato purée and grated cheese in a small bowl.

3. Place two halves of the eggs on each slice of bread and top with the spread. Sprinkle with finely chopped chives and serve together with the tomato salad.

Four servings

10 minutes

6 large tomatoes, diced and marinated in your favourite salad dressing
freshly chopped chives
4 slices rye bread
4 hard-boiled eggs
5 tablespoons sour cream
2 teaspoons tomato purée
4 tablespoons grated Swiss cheese (Emmental cheese)

Waldorf Salad

Four servings
15 minutes

1/4 celeriac
2 tablespoons lemon juice
250 g (8 oz) apples
50 g (1/2 cup) walnuts
1 tin of pineapple chunks
4 tablespoons mayonnaise
salt
sugar
freshly ground white pepper
Worcestershire sauce
6 tablespoons cream

1. Peel the celeriac and cut into fine strips or grate. Sprinkle immediately with lemon juice . Peel the apples, remove the cores and quarter. Cut the quarters into strips or grate. Quarter the walnuts. Mix ingredients carefully together, then drain the pineapple chunks and add them.

2. Mix the mayonnaise with the salt, sugar, pepper and Worcestershire sauce. Whip the cream and fold it into the mayonnaise mixture. Season and stir carefully into the salad.

Tomato Salad with an Open Cheese Sandwich

1. Wash the tomatoes, remove the stalk, cut into slices and arrange on a flat platter. Peel the cloves of garlic and slice into thin slivers. Clean the leeks, wash and cut into thin slices.

2. Wash the parsley, chop finely and sprinkle over the tomatoes. Prepare a dressing with a little salt, freshly ground pepper, vinegar, vegetable stock (broth) and olive oil and pour over the tomatoes. Wash and dry the sprigs of thyme, and garnish the tomatoes with them.

3. Put a slice of cheese or spread some fromage frais on the bread and sprinkle with a little paprika.

One serving

15 minutes

3 tomatoes
1 small clove garlic
1/2 leek
some sprigs of flat leaf parsley
salt
freshly ground black pepper
1 tablespoon white wine vinegar
1–2 tablespoons vegetable stock (broth)
1 teaspoon olive oil
some sprigs of fresh thyme
1 slice ciabatta or other white bread
20 g (3/4 oz) low-fat hard cheese or fromage frais
paprika

Gorgonzola-Salad with Smoked Bacon

Four servings

15 minutes

1 tablespoon olive oil
for frying
10 slices smoked streaky
bacon
150 g (5 oz) Gorgonzola,
crumbled
3 tablespoons olive oil
1 tablespoon lemon juice
mixed salad,
ready packed
salt
Pepper
2 tablespoons pistachio
kernerls,
finely chopped
garlic bread and wine to
serve

1. Heat the olive oil in a pan and fry the bacon until crisp.
Drain on kitchen paper and place to one side.
2. Mix the cheese with the olive oil and lemon juice to a creamy mass. Season with salt and pepper.
3. Mix the salad leaves with the dressing in a bowl. Sprinkle with the bacon and pistachio kernels and lightly mix the salad.
4. Serve with crisp garlic bread and wine.

Greek Country-Style Salad

1. Clean and dice cucumbers and tomatoes and mix together in a large bowl.

2. Dice feta cheese and mix into the tomato-cucumber salad.

3. Combine olive oil, lemon juice, salt and pepper in a small bowl and mix well. Pour over the salad. Mix again, sprinkle the salad with oregano, mix once more and then let it stand for 5 minutes before serving.

Three to four servings

15 minutes

2 large cucumbers
500 g (1 generous pound) tomatoes
250 g (generous 8 oz) feta cheese
50 ml (generous 3 table-spoons) extra virgin olive oil
juice of half a lemon
salt
pepper
oregano

Warm Asparagus Salad

Four servings

15 minutes

1 kg (2 1/4 lb) white asparagus
100 ml / 3 1/2 fl oz (scant 1/2 cup) freshly squeezed orange juice
200 ml / 7 fl oz (7/8 cup) meat stock (broth)
60 g (4 tablespoons) butter
1/2 teaspoon sugar
salt
8 tablespoons oil
6 tablespoons white wine vinegar
4 tomatoes
8 leaves of basil
freshly ground pepper
4 slices Parma ham

1. Peel the asparagus and remove the woody ends. Cut into pieces of 5 cm (2 in) length and place in a pan with a large surface area. Add the orange juice, stock (broth), butter and sugar. Season with salt. Bring quickly to the boil and simmer over a low heat for 10 minutes.

2. Mix the oil and vinegar and add to the asparagus. Cut the tomatoes into eight and the basil into strips. Add to the asparagus and season with pepper.

3. Garnish each plate with a slice of Parma ham.

1. Wash the radishes, top and tail and cut into slices. Wash, top and tail the courgettes and cut into sticks. Wash the fennel bulbs, top and tail and cut diagonally into fine strips. Wash the spring onions (scallions) and chop into slices. Place all these vegetables in a salad bowl.

2. Wash the radish and alfalfa sprouts thoroughly and drain. Add to the vegetables in the salad bowl.

3. Put the lemon juice, pepper, vinegar and stock (broth) in a small bowl and stir to make a smooth mixture. Whisk the thistle oil into this mixture and pour carefully over the vegetables and stir. Allow the salad to stand for 10 minutes. Cut the cress, wash and dry it, and sprinkle over the salad.

Two servings
15 minutes

1 bunch radishes
1 small courgette (zucchini)
1/2 bulb fennel
2 spring onions (scallions)
50 g / 2 oz (1 cup) radish sprouts
50 g / 2 oz (1 cup) alfalfa sprouts
1 tablespoon lemon juice
freshly ground pepper
1 tablespoon white wine vinegar
1 tablespoon vegetable stock (broth)
1 tablespoon thistle oil
1 small box cress

151 Tomato and Rocket Salad

Four servings

15 minutes

100 g (3 1/2 oz) rocket
800 g (1 3/4 lb) medium
sized tomatoes
120 g (1/2 cup) green olives,
stoned (pitted)
2 shallots
1/2 bunch basil
2 tablespoons balsamic
vinegar
2 tablespoons vegetable
stock (broth)
salt
black pepper from the mill
1 teaspoon dried Italian
herbs
1 teaspoon honey
4 tablespoons basil-infused
oil
2 packs mozzarella cheese
(200 g; 7 oz each)
4 slices rye bread

1. Tear the rocket into bite-sized pieces. Cut the tomatoes and drained olives into slices. Peel the shallots and dice very finely. Gently mix these ingredients together in a bowl with a few basil leaves.

2. Pre-heat the oven to 220 °C (425 °F), Gas mark 7.

3. For the salad dressing: mix together the vinegar, vegetable stock (broth), salt, pepper, Italian herbs and honey and stir vigorously. Lastly, add the oil. Pour the dressing over the tomato and rocket salad and mix well.

4. Drain the mozzarella thoroughly, cut into slices and put these on the slices of bread. Sprinkle the remaining basil over the mozzarella and brown under the grill for about 5 minutes.

5. Serve the tomato and rocket salad with the grilled mozzarella-topped slices of bread.

Courgette (Zucchini) and Tomato Salad

1. Hard-boil (hard cook) the eggs, allow to cool and cut into slices. Coarsely chop the parsley. Grate the Parmesan.

2. Peel and slice the courgettes (zucchini). Slice the tomatoes. Put the vegetables into a large bowl.

3. To make the dressing: mix the oil and vinegar, add the sugar and season to taste, stirring well. Pour over the vegetables. Add the sliced eggs and stir very gently.

4. Sprinkle the tomato and courgette (zucchini) salad with parsley and shavings of Parmesan.

Four servings
15 minutes

4 eggs
1 bunch flat leaf parsley
100 g (1 cup) Parmesan
300 g (10 oz) courgettes (zucchini)
500 g (18 oz) plum tomatoes
3 teaspoons balsamic vinegar
5 teaspoons sunflower oil
1 pinch sugar
salt
red pepper from the mill

153 Asparagus and Strawberry Salad

Four servings
20 minutes

400 g (14 oz) green
asparagus
salt
sugar
60 ml (6 tablespoons) strawberry vinegar
60 ml (6 tablespoons) sunflower oil
freshly ground white pepper
160 g (6 oz) fresh straw-
berries

1. Wash the asparagus, remove the woody ends and cook briefly in boiling water, seasoned with salt, sugar and 5 tablespoons of vinegar. Simmer for 5 minutes over a low heat. Remove the asparagus and rinse in ice cold water to cool it down quickly. Arrange in a flat gratin dish.

2. Make a marinade with 6 tablespoons of the asparagus water, 1 tablespoon vinegar, oil, salt, pepper and a pinch of sugar. Pour over the asparagus, coating it all over with the marinade. Leave to stand.

3. Clean and wash the strawberries. Purée 40 g / 1 1/2 oz strawberries. Cut the remaining ones into quarters and sprinkle with sugar so that the fruit produce a little juice. Mix the strawberry purée and strawberry pieces and add to the asparagus. Stir again.

1. Place fish in tomato sauce into a bowl and carefully cut the fillets into small pieces.
2. Chop the onion, slice the pickle thinly and dice the eggs.
3. Add all the chopped ingredients to the fish. Stir and then season with pepper and thyme.
4. Allow the salad to cool for a while. Then place on toast before serving.

Two servings
20 minutes

2 tins herring fillets in tomato sauce
1 small onion
1 small pickle
2 hard-boiled eggs
pepper
thyme
4 slices of bread, lightly toasted

155

Gratiné Goat's Cheese on a Melon Bed

Two servings

20 minutes

80 g (3 oz) mangetout (snow peas)
2 young carrots
50 ml (3 tablespoons) chicken stock (broth)
1/2 ripe honeydew melon
2 small goat's cheeses (each 50 g; 2 oz)
1/2 teaspoon fresh thyme leaves
2 teaspoons maple syrup
1 teaspoon medium strength mustard
1 tablespoon cider vinegar
herb salt
freshly ground pepper
1 teaspoon capers
1 teaspoon walnut oil
2 tablespoons chopped walnuts or 1 slice Parma ham

1. Wash and prepare the mangetout (snow peas). Cut the pods in half. Peel the carrots and cut them into thin slices. Heat the chicken stock (broth) and cook the vegetables in it for about 5 minutes. Drain them and reserve the cooking liquid.

2. Preheat the oven to 200°C (400°F), Gas mark 6. Remove the seeds from the melon, cut into slices and peel. Place the cheeses in a small ovenproof dish, sprinkle with thyme and pour 1 teaspoon maple syrup on top. Bake in the oven for about 10 minutes until they begin to melt.

3. Mix the mustard, remaining maple syrup, cider vinegar, 1 tablespoon stock (broth), herb salt, pepper and capers together to make a dressing and whisk in the walnut oil.

4. Arrange the salad and melon slices on two plates and put the cheeses on top. Pour the dressing over the salad. Sprinkle chopped walnuts on top or cut Parma ham into strips and garnish the salad with them.

Rocket Salad with Chicken Breasts

1. Sprinkle lemon juice over the chicken breasts and season them with freshly ground pepper. Heat the sunflower oil in a non-stick pan and fry the chicken breasts for about 5 minutes on each side. Remove from the pan. Leave to cool and cut into strips.

2. Wash and dry the rocket and lamb's lettuce. Wash and prepare the pepper, cut into thin strips and put in a large bowl together with the salad. Mix the olive oil, mustard, vinegar, pepper and chopped chives to make a dressing. Pour over the salad and stir.

3. Arrange the salad on two plates, put the chicken strips on top and sprinkle with Parmesan.

Two servings

20 minutes

2 chicken breast fillets
1 teaspoon lemon juice
freshly ground pepper
1 teaspoon sunflower oil
150 g (5 oz) rocket
50 g (2 oz) lamb's lettuce
1 red sweet pepper
1 teaspoon olive oil
1 teaspoon mustard
1 tablespoon white wine vinegar
1 tablespoon chopped chives
1 tablespoon freshly grated Parmesan

157

Romain Salad with Cottage Cheese Puffs

Four servings

10 minutes

Romain lettuce mixed with some mustard green topped with your favourite dressing
2 eggs
1/8 l (1/2 cup) milk
375 g (scant 1 3/4 cups) cottage cheese (small curd)
100 g (generous 3/4 cup) flour
50 g (scant 1/2 cup) cornflour
1 teaspoon baking powder
1/2 tablespoon chopped caraway
1 small onion, finely chopped
oil for sautéing
salt
1 teaspoon baking powder
freshly chopped chives

1. Mix eggs, milk and cottage cheese very well and then press the mixture through a sieve.

2. Sift flour; cornflour and baking powder into the cottage cheese mixture and season well with caraway and onion.

3. Heat some oil in a pan and spoon in portions of the batter. Sauté puffs until golden brown on both sides.

4. Sprinkle the puffs with the freshly chopped chives and serve with the lettuce.

Asparagus Salad with a Vinaigrette Dressing

1. Wash the asparagus, remove the woody ends and simmer in gently boiling water seasoned with lemon juice, sugar and salt for about 10 minutes. Remove the asparagus from the water and leave to cool.

2. Hard-boil (hard-cook) the eggs, shell and separate the yolks from the whites. Chop the egg whites finely and put to one side. Crush the egg yolks with a fork, add to the 2 raw egg yolks and stir in the olive oil, vinegar, mustard, capers and red wine. Season with salt and pepper.

3. Wash and dry the parsley and the chervil. Chop finely and stir into the vinaigrette together with the chopped egg white.

4. Arrange the asparagus on a dish and pour the vinaigrette over it.

Four servings

20 minutes

1 kg (2 1/4 lb) green asparagus
1 tablespoon lemon juice
1 pinch sugar
1 pinch salt
4 eggs
yolks of 2 eggs
2 tablespoons olive oil
1 tablespoon wine vinegar
1 1/2 teaspoon Dijon mustard
2 teaspoons capers
4 tablespoons red wine
freshly ground pepper
salt
30 g (1 oz) parsley
chervil to taste

159

Tofu (Bean Curd) Salad with Asparagus

Four servings

20 minutes

450 g (1 lb) green asparagus
5 tablespoons soy sauce
juice and zest of 1/2 untreated lemon
3 teaspoons sugar
5 tablespoons sunflower oil
300 g (11 oz) tofu (bean curd)
1 spring onion (scallion)
1 red onion
30 g (1 oz) watercress
piece of fresh ginger, about 3 cm (1 1/4 in) long

1. Wash the asparagus, remove the woody ends. Cut off the asparagus tips and keep them separate. Cut the rest into pieces of 5 cm/2 in length. Bring water to the boil with 1 tablespoon of soya sauce and cook the asparagus tips for 3 minutes. Remove from the water, drain and put to one side. Add the rest of the pieces to the water and cook for 5 minutes, then drain.

2. To make the salad dressing: mix 4 tablespoons soy sauce, lemon juice, grated lemon zest, sugar and sunflower oil and stir well.

3. Cut the tofu (bean curd) into cubes. Wash and trim the spring onion (scallion). Peel the red onion. Cut both into rings. Pull the leaves off the watercress. Mix all the ingredients with the asparagus pieces, stirring very carefully.

4. Peel the ginger, grate finely and sprinkle over the salad. Garnish with the asparagus tips.

Salad of Asparagus Tips and Mangetouts (snow peas)

1. Wash the asparagus tips and cut once lengthways. Wash and prepare the mangetouts (snow peas) and cook together with the asparagus in a small amount of gently boiling water until done.

2. Wash the salad leaves and arrange on four plates; place the asparagus tips and mangetouts (snow peas) on top. Mix the olive oil, balsamic vinegar, salt and pepper and sprinkle over the salad, asparagus and mangetouts (snow peas).

3. Slice shavings of Parmesan and sprinkle over the salad, asparagus and mangetouts (snow peas). Garnish with watercress.

Four servings

10 minutes

500 g (18 oz) green asparagus tips
400 g (14 oz) mangetouts (snow peas)
250 g (9 oz) coloured salad leaves
5 tablespoons olive oil
1 tablespoon balsamic vinegar
salt
freshly ground pepper
80 g / 3 oz (1/2 cup) Parmesan, shaved
watercress for garnish

161

Pasta and Courgette (Zucchini) Salad

Two servings

20 minutes

salt
50 g (2 oz) wholemeal
(wholewheat) pasta
1 small courgette (zucchini)
3 large mushrooms
1 tablespoon lemon juice
1 tablespoon white wine
1 tablespoon low-fat salad
cream
freshly ground pepper
5 cashew nuts

1. Bring 1 litre (4 1/2 cups) water to the boil in a saucepan. Add the wholemeal (wholewheat) pasta and season with a pinch of salt. Cook the pasta "al dente" and drain.
2. Wash and top and tail the courgette. Prepare the mushrooms and wipe them very carefully with kitchen paper. Cut both into fine slices. Make a dressing with lemon juice, white wine, salad cream and pepper.
3. Put the pasta in a small salad bowl and add the mushrooms and courgettes (zucchini). Pour over the dressing and stir to coat all the ingredients. Coarsely chop the cashew nuts and sprinkle over the pasta salad.

1. Put the fish fillets in a shallow saucepan or frying pan, sprinkle with a little lemon juice and add 2 tablespoons water. Cover and cook the fish gently for about 5–10 minutes. Remove the pan from the heat, take out the fish and leave to cool on a plate.

2. Wash and prepare the fennel bulbs, remove the green leaves and put to one side. Cut the fennel into small pieces. Wash and prepare the spring onions (scallions) and chop into small pieces.

3. Put the pepper, white wine vinegar, salad cream, curry powder and 1–2 tablespoons cooking liquid into a bowl and stir well to obtain a smooth, spicy dressing.

4. Place the vegetables in a serving bowl, shred the fish fillet coarsely with a fork and arrange on top of the vegetables. Pour the dressing over the vegetables and fish and stir carefully. Leave to stand for a few minutes and garnish with fennel leaves. Serve with a wholemeal (wholewheat) bread roll.

Four servings
25 minutes

100 g (3 1/2 oz) low-fat sea fish fillet (for instance cod or pollack)
2 tablespoons lemon juice
1/2 bulb fennel with leaves
1 spring onion (scallion)
freshly ground white pepper
1 tablespoon white wine vinegar
2 tablespoons low-fat salad cream
1 pinch curry powder
1 wholemeal (wholewheat) bread roll

163

Potato Salad with Herbal Yoghurt Dressing

Two servings

25 minutes

400 g (14 oz) small waxy
potatoes
1 apple
1 teaspoon lemon juice
1 small courgette (zucchini)
1 small onion
1/2 bunch radishes
70 g / 3 oz (1/3 cup) low-fat
yoghurt (1.5%)
1 tablespoon low-fat
mayonnaise
1 tablespoon white wine
vinegar
sea salt
freshly ground pepper
1 bunch chives
2 tablespoons cress
50 g (2 oz) rocket

1. Put the potatoes in a steamer. Fill the
bottom with water and steam for about 20–
25 minutes until tender. Peel and cut into
quarters.
2. Peel the apple, cut into eight pieces and
remove the core. Sprinkle lemon juice on the
apple pieces. Wash, top and tail the courgette
(zucchini) and slice finely. Peel the onions and
chop finely. Wash the radishes, top and tail and
slice. Arrange the potatoes, sliced fruit and
vegetables on two plates.
3. Stir the yoghurt and salad cream together
and season with vinegar, salt and pepper.
Wash the chives and chop finely. Wash and dry
the cress and rocket, and chop coarsely. Add
the herbs to the yoghurt and salad cream mixture and pour over the vegetables.

Potato Salad à la South Germany

1. Place the potatoes in a pot with salted water and bring to a boil. Lower the heat and simmer for 10 minutes. Pour off the water.

2. Bring the chicken broth to a boil and pour over the potatoes. Mix well.

3. In the meantime heat the oil in a pan and sauté the bacon until crisp. Take out the bacon and drain well.

4. Combine mustard, honey and vinegar in a small bowl. Mix into the potatoes.

5. Stir in the bacon with the onions and season with salt and pepper.

Four servings
25 minutes

1 kg (generous 2 pounds) potatoes, peeled and sliced
250 ml (1 cup) chicken broth
1 tablespoon oil
100 g (scant 4 oz) smoked streaky bacon, diced
1 tablespoon mustard, medium hot
2 tablespoons honey
40 ml (2 1/2 tablespoons) cider vinegar
50 g / 2 oz (generous 1/3 cup) onions, diced
salt
pepper

Tabbouleh

Four servings

25 minutes

250 g / 9 oz (1 1/4 cup)
buckwheat
4 large ripe tomatoes
2 bunches of flat leaf
parsley, finely chopped
2 large bunches of mint,
finely chopped
2 Shallots, finely chopped
4 tablespoons olive oil
2 tablespoons lemon juice
salt
pepper
to serve:
warm unleavened bread
4 hard boiled eggs

1. Briefly roast the buckwheat, then leave to
soak in water for 15–20 minutes.
2. deseed and finely chop the tomatoes.
and mix with the buckwheat and the other
ingredients in a bowl. Season with salt and
pepper.
3. Serve with warm unleavened bread and
peeled hard boiled eggs.

Asparagus Salad with New Potatoes

1. Wash the potatoes and boil in their skins. Wash the asparagus and remove the woody ends. Cut the asparagus into pieces of 2 cm / 3/4 in length and cook in 250 ml/8 fl oz (1 cup) salted boiling water for about 10 minutes until done. Remove from the water and drain.

2. Bring the asparagus water back to the boil. Pour 2 or 3 tablespoons of it over the peeled, finely chopped onion in the salad bowl, discarding the rest. Shell the hard-boiled egg, dice it and add to the onion mixture. Mix the vinegar, oil, salt and pepper to make a marinade. Pour into the salad bowl and stir well.

3. Peel the potatoes and cut into slices; add them still hot to the marinade.

4. Carefully mix together the washed, finely chopped parsley, asparagus and potatoes.

Four servings
30 minutes

1 kg (2 1/4 lb) new potatoes
500 g (18 oz) green asparagus
salt
1 onion
1 soft-boiled (soft-cooked) egg
2 tablespoons vinegar
2 tablespoons olive oil
freshly ground pepper
1 bunch parsley

Melon and Orange Salad

Two servings

30 minutes

1/4 watermelon
1 orange
1 teaspoon orange liqueur
1/2 teaspoon cinnamon
1 teaspoon honey
1 tablespoon lemon juice
1 tablespoon walnuts

1. Peel the watermelon, remove the seeds and cut the flesh into small cubes. Peel the orange and cut into segments. Cut the orange segments in half and put in a bowl with the diced melon.

2. Mix the orange liqueur, cinnamon, honey and lemon juice together. Pour it over the fruit salad and stir well. Put in a cool place and leave to stand for about 30 minutes. Coarsely chop the walnuts and sprinkle over the melon and orange salad.

One Thousand and One Nights Salad

1. Wash the apples thoroughly, remove the cores and quarter. Cut the quarters into thin julienne strips. Sprinkle with the lemon juice.

2. Wash the dates, cut in half and remove the stones. Cut into fine strips and mix together in a bowl with the apples.

3. Put the marzipan, orange blossom water and yoghurt in a bowl and stir to a smooth paste.

4. Pre-heat oven to 180 °C (350 °F), gas mark 4.

5. Place the almonds on a baking tray and roast in the pre-heated oven until they are golden brown. Turn occasionally.

6. Wash the figs, remove the stalks and cut a cross in the top. Press the lower half of the fruit together with thumb and finger to make it open up like a blossom.

7. Arrange the apple and date mixture on four plates. Place a fig on each one, spoon the yoghurt and orange blossom filling into the middle of each fig, and decorate with a roast almond.

Four servings
30 minutes

700 g (1 1/2 lb) untreated eating apples
juice of 1/2 lemon
175 g (6 1/2 oz) fresh dates
25 g (2 tablespoons) white marzipan
1 teaspoon orange blossom water
4 tablespoons plain yoghurt
4 peeled almonds
4 fresh, green figs

169 Indian Rice Salad

Two servings

30 minutes

100 g (3 1/2 oz) cooked rice
(about 30–40 g or 1–1 1/2 oz
(ca. 1/4 cup) uncooked
weight)
50 g (2 oz) cooked chicken
breast
2 spring onions (scallions)
1 small piece root ginger
1 tablespoon lemon juice
1 tablespoon vegetable
stock (broth)
1 tablespoon soy sauce
1/2 teaspoon curry powder
1 pinch chilli powder
1 teaspoon sesame seeds
1 apricot
some mint leaves

1. Put the cooked brown rice in a bowl. Cut the chicken breast into strips, wash and prepare the spring onions (scallions), chop finely and add both to the rice.

2. Peel the ginger, grate it finely and add to the lemon juice, vegetable stock (broth), soy sauce, curry and chilli powder. Stir to make a dressing and pour over the rice and chicken. Mix thoroughly and leave to stand for a few minutes.

3. Fry the sesame seeds in a non-stick frying pan without any oil and sprinkle over the rice. Cut the apricot in half, remove the stone (pit), peel and cut into slices. Garnish the rice with the apricot slices and mint leaves.

1. Heat salted water in a saucepan. Wash and prepare the lemon grass, cut to length and add to the salted water together with the wild rice which should be cooked according to the instructions on the packet. Drain, leave to cool and remove the lemon grass.

2. Sprinkle lime juice over the crabmeat. Wash and prepare the pepper and cut into thin strips. Peel the shallots and chop finely. Add the crabmeat, strips of pepper and chopped shallot to the cooled rice and stir very carefully.

3. Peel the ginger, chop finely and place in a small bowl. Add the sesame oil, soy sauce and cayenne pepper, stir well and pour this mixture over the rice salad. Leave the salad to stand for about 20 minutes. Wash the coriander and chop it finely. Also chop the peanuts finely. Sprinkle both on the rice salad.

Two servings

30 minutes

salt
2 stems lemon grass
80 g / 3 oz (1/2 cup) wild rice
120 g / 4 oz (1/2 cup) cooked crab meat
1 tablespoon lime juice
1 red sweet pepper
1 shallot
1 small piece fresh root ginger
1 teaspoon sesame oil
1 teaspoon soy sauce
cayenne pepper
1 tablespoon fresh coriander leaves
1 tablespoon peanuts

Bok Choy, Vietnamese

Four servings
10 minutes

2 tablespoons thistle oil
2 stems of lemon grass, finely chopped
1 teaspoon grated ginger
2 red chili peppers, finely chopped
1 clove garlic, pressed
1 shallot, diced
1 tablespoon honey
1 tablespoon fish sauce
1 kg (generous 2 pounds) young bok choy, cut in half lengthwise
2 tablespoons rice wine

1. Heat the oil in a deep pan. Add the lemon grass, ginger, chili peppers, garlic, shallots, honey and fish sauce. Sauté the mixture for about 2 minutes, stirring constantly.
2. Add the bok choy with 1/4 cup of water. Allow to simmer for a while until the leaves begin to fall apart. Stir in the rice wine and serve immediately.

Sausage with Mashed Potatoes

1. Prepare the mashed potatoes according to the directions on the packet, but use milk instead of water! Stir in the butter and season with salt and grated nutmeg.

2. In the meantime heat oil in a frying pan. Cut into the sausages 3 or 4 times on each side and then place in the skillet. Brown on each side for 2 minutes and then remove them. Add crème fraîche to the oil in the pan and mix well. Season the sauce as desired with salt, pepper and a little red wine.

Four servings

10 minutes

1 packet (for 4 persons) mashed potato flakes
1/2 l (2 cups) milk
1 tablespoon butter
salt
grated nutmeg (as desired)
4 tablespoons oil
4 knackwurst or similar sausages
100 g / 3 1/2 oz (1/2 cup) crème fraîche
a bit of red wine (as desired)

Root Vegetables with Pumpkin Seed Oil

Two servings
10 minutes

1/2 celeriac
3 carrots
1 parsley root
1/2 kohlrabi
1 teaspoon lemon juice
sea salt
freshly ground multi-coloured pepper
1 tablespoon white wine vinegar
2 teaspoons pumpkin seed oil
1 tablespoon cashew nuts

1. Wash, prepare and peel the celeriac, carrots, parsley root and kohlrabi. Using a vegetable grater, grate into thin strips. Put the vegetables in a large bowl.

2. Mix together the lemon juice, sea salt, multi-coloured pepper and white wine vinegar to make a dressing. Finally, add the pumpkin seed oil and stir carefully with a fork.

3. Pour the dressing over the raw vegetables and leave to stand for a few minutes. Coarsely chop the cashew nuts and sprinkle over the vegetables. Serve with unleavened bread.

174

Herrings fillets with Cottage Cheese Remoulade

1. Stir cottage cheese until smooth and add milk and oil bit by bit.

2. Dice the pickle and 1 herring fillet. Mix them into the cottage cheese and season with salt, pepper and herbs.

3. Serve the remoulade with the remaining fillets. They taste best served with boiled potatoes.

Four servings
10 minutes

250 g (1 generous cup) cottage cheese (small curd)
1/4 l (1 cup) milk
4 tablespoons olive oil
1 pickle
5 herring fillets
salt
pepper
fresh, finely chopped herbs

175

Liptau Cottage Cheese Remoulade

Two servings
10 minutes

65 g (1/4 cup) butter
250 g (1 cup) cottage cheese
1/2 teaspoon salt
1/2 teaspoon rose paprika
anchovy paste from the tube
1/2 tablespoon mustard
fresh chive

1. Stir the butter until creamy, then add the cottage cheese and all the other ingredients. Mix well. Serve with the freshly boiled potatoes.

176

Raw Vegetables with Yoghurt Dip

Two servings

10 minutes

Various vegetables (for example, cocktail tomatoes, green peppers, carrots, fennel and radishes) cut into finger-size pieces
500 g / 17 oz (2 cups) natural yoghurt
1 tablespoon lemon juice
salt
2 tablespoons mayonnaise
fresh, finely chopped herbs

1. Mix yoghurt, lemon juice, salt and mayonnaise with a whisk. Then add the chopped herbs and stir. Serve the yoghurt dip in a small bowl together with the raw vegetable platter.

Pig's Liver with Apples and Mashed Potatoes

1. Prepare mashed potatoes according to the directions on the packet, using milk instead of water! Mix in the butter and season with salt and nutmeg.

2. In the meantime sprinkle the flour onto a flat plate and mix with salt and pepper. Clean the pig's liver, pat dry and coat with flour. Remove the cores from the apples and cut into thick rings.

3. Heat oil in a pan and fry the livers on each side for 1–2 minutes. Be careful that they don't dry out. Remove from the pan and put in the apple rings. Sauté them also for 1–2 minutes, being careful they don't fall apart. Garnish the livers with the apple rings and serve.

Four servings

10 minutes

Flaked mashed potatoes
(packet for 4 persons)
1/2 l (2 cups) milk
1 tablespoon butter
salt
nutmeg (as desired)
2 tablespoons flour
salt and pepper
4 pieces pig's liver
2 tablespoons oil
2 apples
juice of 1/2 lemon

178 Spaghetti in Garlic Oil

Two servings

10 minutes

500 g (1 generous pound) spaghetti
7 tablespoons extra virgin olive oil
4 tablespoons butter
3 large cloves garlic, finely chopped
1 tablespoon oregano
30 g (1 oz) grated Parmesan

1. Bring a pot of salted water to a boil. Add the spaghetti and 1 tablespoon of the olive oil and cook for about 7 minutes until al dente. Drain.

2. In the meantime heat the butter in a small sauce pan, add the garlic and let it brown slightly. Remove the pan from the heat, add the remaining olive oil and mix with the butter.

3. Place the noodles into bowls, sprinkle with the garlic oil and top with oregano and Parmesan.

179 Spaghetti Pesto

1. Prepare spaghetti as above. Add pesto to spagetti and mix well.

Four servings

10 minutes

500 g (1 generous pound) spaghetti
1 tablespoon extra virgin olive oil (as desired)
1 glass of pesto (185 g; 6 oz)

Spinach with Boiled Potatoes and Fried Eggs

1. Clean potatoes thoroughly and steam in a pressure cooker until done.

2. In the meantime wash the spinach and place into a pot, setting about 1/5 of the leaves aside. Quickly bring the spinach to boil in the water and afterwards strain well.

3. Peel the onions and chop finely together with the spinach in the food processor.

4. Heat the butter in a pot, add the flour and milk und stir until smooth. Add the spinach and let it cook for 3 minutes (not longer) while continuing to stir.

5. In the meantime heat a bit of butter in the pan and fry 4 eggs sunny side up.

6. Season the spinach with salt, pepper and nutmeg and stir in the raw spinach that you set aside before.

Four servings
10 minutes

12 medium-sized potatoes
1 kg (generous 2 pounds) spinach
125 ml (1/2 cup) water
2 onions
50 g (3 generous table-spoons) butter
30 g (1/4 cup) flour
250 ml (1 cup) milk
butter for frying
4 eggs
salt
pepper
nutmeg

181

Spinach with mashed Potatoes and Fried Eggs

Four servings
10 minutes

see recipe 180

1. Children like this recipe better if you serve mashed potatoes instead of boiled potatoes. Prepare the mashed potatoes according to the directions on the package but use milk instead of water and add a bit of butter and salt.

182

Hunters' apples

1. Wash the apples thoroughly. Cut off a "lid", remove the cores and partially hollow out the apples. Cut the game into small pieces.
2. Peel the celeriac and grate finely. Put in a bowl with the pieces of meat and mix with the cranberry jelly and mayonnaise.
3. Fill the apples with the mixture and put the lids back on.

Four servings
10 minutes

4 apples
200 g (7 oz) cooked game
1 small celeriac
1 tablespoon cranberry jelly
1 tablespoon mayonnaise

Fried Asparagus with Pork Chops

183

1. Peel the asparagus and remove the woody ends. Cut the asparagus into pieces of 4 cm/ 1 1/2 in length. Rinse the lemons in hot water and wipe dry. Peel half the lemon thinly and cut the zest into thin strips.

2. Cut the meat into thin strips, fry in hot oil, add the asparagus and fry for 3–4 minutes, stirring constantly. Add 2 tablespoons lemon juice and season with salt and pepper. Add the lemon zest and finely chopped chives.

Four servings

10 minutes

1.2 kg (2 1/2 lb) white asparagus
1 untreated lemon
600 g (1 1/4 lb) boned pork chops
3 tablespoons oil
5 tablespoons soya sauce
salt
freshly ground pepper
1 bunch chives

184

Tagliatelle with Asparagus and Broccoli

Four servings

10 minutes

250 g (9 oz) white asparagus
400 g (14 oz) broccoli
2 cloves garlic
50 g (4 tablespoons) butter
salt
freshly ground pepper
250 g (9 oz) mascarpone
250 g (9 oz) tagliatelle

1. Peel the asparagus, remove the woody ends and cut into pieces of 2 cm / 3/4 in length. Clean and wash the broccoli and separate the florets. Peel the cloves of garlic and chop finely. Add to the broccoli and asparagus and braise lightly in the butter. Cover and cook over a low heat for 4 minutes. Season with salt and butter. Add the mascarpone, stir well and cook until the sauce becomes creamy.

2. Cook the tagliatelle al dente in 2–3 litres/ (9–13 cups) of boiling water. Pour away the water and drain. Arrange the tagliatelle on plates and garnish with the vegetables.

Tagliatelle with Spinach

1. Bring a large saucepan of salted water to the boil and cook the tagliatelle "al dente" following the instructions on the packet. Remove any damaged leaves and coarse stalks and wash the spinach. Peel the shallots and garlic and chop finely. Fry the pine kernels until golden yellow.

2. Heat the olive oil in a pan and fry the shallots until golden brown, add the garlic and fry briefly. Add the spinach, let it collapse, cover and cook gently over a low flame for about 3 minutes. Add the milk, bring to the boil and stir in the sauce thickening. Cook until the sauce has thickened, stirring all the time. Season the spinach with herb salt, pepper and a touch of nutmeg.

3. Drain the tagliatelle and arrange with the spinach on two warmed plates. Sprinkle with the fried pine kernels and Pecorino cheese.

Two servings
15 minutes

sea salt
300 g (10 oz) tagliatelle
300 g (10 oz) fresh leaf spinach
2 shallots
2 cloves garlic
1 tablespoon pine kernels
2 teaspoons olive oil
100 ml (1/2 cup) low-fat milk (1.5%)
1 teaspoon sauce thickening
herb salt
freshly ground pepper
freshly grated nutmeg
30 g (1 cup) grated Pecorino cheese

186

Farfalle with Broccoli

Für 1 Person

15 minutes

salt
200 g (7 oz) broccoli
50 g (2 oz) farfalle
1 clove garlic
coarse sea salt
chilli pepper
a few white peppercorns
2 anchovy fillets (preserved in oil)
some fresh basil leaves

1. Bring about 1 litre (4 1/2 cups) water to the boil in a large saucepan and add a little salt.

2. Wash and prepare the broccoli and divide into small florets. Put the broccoli and pasta in the boiling water and cook until the pasta is ready.

3. Peel the garlic and put in a mortar with a little sea salt, the chilli powder, peppercorns and anchovy fillets and crush to make a paste. Take 2–3 tablespoons of the pasta-broccoli cooking liquid and stir into the paste.

4. Drain the pasta and broccoli, arrange on a plate and stir in the spicy sauce. Wash and dry the basil leaves, and garnish the pasta and broccoli.

Shrimps with Radicchio and Tomatoes

1. Quarter the tomatoes, remove the seeds and chop up. Cut the radicchio into fine strips.

2. Heat the oil in a large pan and briefly fry the shrimps on all sides. Add the radicchio and tomatoes, stir and cover. Cook over a low flame for about 8 minutes, stirring occasionally. Season with salt, pepper and lemon juice.

Four servings
15 minutes

2 medium tomatoes
2 small chicory heads
4 tablespoons garlic-infused oil
24 large prawns (shrimps), peeled and without heads
salt
white pepper
lemon juice

Wok-fried Vegetables

Two servings

15 minutes

1 red sweet pepper
1/2 celeriac
1 carrot
100 g (3 1/2 oz) mushrooms
2 spring onions (scallions)
100 g (3 1/2 oz) fresh soy sauce
1 small piece fresh root ginger
1 clove garlic
1 tablespoon groundnut oil
200 ml (7/8 cup) vegetable stock
3 tablespoons soy sauce
1 teaspoon cornflour (corn starch)
1 pinch chilli pepper
1 teaspoon lemon juice
freshly ground pepper

1. Wash and prepare the pepper and cut into thin strips. Peel the celeriac and carrots and cut into thin sticks. Wash and prepare the spring onions (scallions) and cut into rings. Wash the bean sprouts and drain.

2. Peel the ginger and garlic and chop finely. Heat the groundnut oil in the wok and briefly fry the ginger and garlic but do not allow to brown. Add the vegetables and mushrooms and fry for about 3–5 minutes, stirring continuously. The vegetables should remain crisp.

3. Stir together the vegetable stock , soy sauce and cornflour (corn starch). Pour over the vegetables and bring briefly to the boil. Season with chilli, lemon juice and pepper.

Green Asparagus with Parmesan Shavings

1. Fry the Parma ham until crisp. Remove from the pan, leave to cool and cut into strips.

2. Wash the asparagus and remove the woody ends. Cook in salted water for about 10 minutes until done. Remove from the water, drain and arrange on plates.

3. Mix the olive oil, vinegar, salt and pepper to make the dressing. Stir well and pour over the asparagus. Garnish with the Parma ham and Parmesan shavings.

Four servings
15 minutes

4 slices Parma ham
1 kg (2 1/4 lb) green asparagus
salt
2 tablespoons olive oil
1 teaspoon vinegar
freshly ground pepper
60 g (2 oz) Parmesan cheese, shaved

Asparagus with Veal Quenelles in Cream Sauce

Four servings

15 minutes

2 kg (4 1/2 lb) white asparagus
salt
40 g (3 tablespoons) butter
600 g (1 1/4 lb) minced (ground) veal
450 ml / 15 fl oz (2 cups) cream
freshly ground white pepper
1 level tablespoon flour
1 bunch parsley

1. Peel the asparagus, remove the woody ends and cut into pieces of 3 cm / 1 1/4 in length. Cook in boiling salted water with 1 tablespoon butter for 10 minutes until tender. Remove from the water and keep in a warm place. Stir 1 glass of cream into the minced (ground) veal to make a smooth mixture. Season with salt and pepper.

2. Heat the remaining butter, stir in the flour and add a little asparagus stock to make a creamy sauce. Add the remaining cream and reduce the sauce a little to thicken it. Season with salt and pepper. Add the asparagus and three-quarters of the finely chopped parsley.

3. Heat the asparagus stock . Form the veal quenelles with a spoon and simmer very gently in the asparagus stock over a low heat. Arrange the asparagus on the plates with the veal quenelles around it. Pour the sauce on top garnish with the rest of the herbs.

Rabbit Fillet with Green Asparagus

1. Wash the asparagus and remove the woody ends. Cut the asparagus stalks (stems) into pieces of 7 cm / 2 3/4 in length. Heat 2 tablespoons groundnut oil and fry the asparagus in it. Season with salt, pepper, 1 scant tablespoon Oriental mixed herbs and 2 scant tablespoons sesame oil.

2. Wash the rabbit fillets, wipe dry, season with salt and pepper and fry in the remaining oil.

3. Add the chilli sauce, a small amount of Oriental mixed herbs, a few drops of sesame oil and coconut pulp to the mayonnaise and stir to make a smooth mixture.

4. Put some mayonnaise on four plates and arrange the asparagus and rabbit fillet on top. Garnish with coriander (cilantro) and sesame seeds.

Four servings
15 minutes

1 kg (2 1/4 lb) green asparagus
5 tablespoons groundnut oil
salt
freshly ground pepper
1 tablespoon Oriental mixed herbs
2 tablespoons sesame oil
4 rabbit fillets (about 100 g; 3 1/2 oz each)
125 g (4 1/2 oz) mayonnaise
a few drops of chilli sauce
125 g (4 1/2 oz) coconut pulp
1/2 tablespoon fresh coriander (cilantro) as garnish
black sesame seeds as garnish

Macaroni with Walnut Sauce

Four servings

15 minutes

200 g (7 oz) macaroni
4 tablespoons olive oil
3 cloves garlic, finely chopped
150 g / 5 oz (1 cup) walnuts, chopped
200 g / 7 oz (1 scant cup) ricotta
75 g (2 1/2 oz) parsley, finely chopped
250 ml / 8 fl oz (1 cup) crème fraîche
salt
pepper
nutmeg
walnut halves

1. Bring plenty of salted water to a boil and then pour in the macaroni. Cook according to the directions on the package until al dente. Drain. Set aside 1 cup of noodle water.

2. In the meantime heat 1 tablespoon olive oil in a frying pan and brown the garlic. Mix the walnuts, Ricotta, parsley, garlic and crème fraîche with 3 tablespoons of olive oil.

3. Place the mixture into a small pot. Heat the mixture while continuing to stir and thin it with some of the noodle water. Season with salt, pepper and nutmeg.

4. Garnish with walnut halves before serving..

Country Style Boiled Potatoes

1. Wash the potatoes and cook in a pressure cooker until done. Serve with butter, Limburg cheese, Harz cheese and chives. Serve with fresh milk to drink.

Four servings
15 minutes

12 medium-sized potatoes

To serve:
butter
Limburg cheese
Harz cheese
chives, finely chopped
fresh milk (to drink)

Raw Vegetables with Cottage Cheese Balls

Four servings
15 minutes

Various vegetables (for example, green peppers, carrots, cocktail tomatoes, radishes and fennel) cut into bite-size pieces
50 g (3 tablespoons) butter
50 g (2 oz) grated cheese
250 g (9 oz) cottage cheese (small curd)
salt, rose paprika (mild)
100 g (4 oz) pumpernickel

1. Stir the butter until creamy. Add the cheese and cottage cheese and season with salt and paprika.
2. Chop the pumpernickel in fine pieces.
3. Using 2 teaspoons, form walnut-sized balls of cottage cheese-cheese mixture and roll in the diced pumpernickel.
4. Arrange the cheese balls decoratively between the raw vegetables on a platter and serve.

195

Raw Vegetable Platter with Beef Liver

Four servings

15 minutes

Ingredients and preparation are the same as in the previous recipe apart from:
4 slices beef liver
salt
pepper
juice of 1/2 lemon
2 tablespoons olive oil

1. Pat the liver dry; then sprinkle with salt, pepper and lemon juice.

2. Heat oil in the pan and fry the liver on both sides 1–2 minutes. The outside should be crisp but the inside raw.

3. Serve together with the raw vegetables and baguette rolls.

1. Peel the white asparagus, wash the green asparagus, remove the woody ends. Cook the asparagus for about 20 minutes in gently simmering salted watering together with sugar and butter.

2. Peel the shallot and chop coarsely. Chop up the gherkin. Purée the chopped shallot and gherkin with the mixed herbs, yoghurt and 1 tablespoon of oil. Season with salt, mustard and cayenne pepper.

3. Separate the eggs. Mix the egg yolks, chives and pepper and fold into the egg whites which have been stiffly beaten. Make four omelettes, one after the other.

4. Remove the asparagus from the water, drain and arrange on one half of the omelette. Fold the other half over the asparagus. Pour the herb sauce over the omelette and garnish with chervil leaves.

Four servings

15 minutes

600 g (1 1/4 lb) white asparagus
600 g (1 1/4 lb) green asparagus
salt
1 pinch sugar
1 teaspoon butter
1 shallot
1 gherkin
25 g (1 oz) mixed herbs
150 g / 5 1/2 oz (2/3 cups) yoghurt
5 tablespoons oil
1 teaspoon mustard
cayenne pepper
6 eggs
2 tablespoons milk
1 tablespoon chives
freshly ground pepper
a few chervil leaves

Knuckles of Pork with Onions and Vegetables

Four servings

15 minutes

250 g (9 oz) pork fillet
(tenderloin)
salt
freshly ground pepper
1 teaspoon cooking oil
2 peaches
2 tablespoons peach
preserve
1 teaspoon white wine
vinegar
1 teaspoon soy sauce
1 mild red chilli pepper

1. Pour boiling water over the tomatoes, peel and slice them. Peel the onions and cut them into slices also.

2. Heat the oil in a pot and simmer the tomato and onion slices.

3. Mix the flour with the heavy cream and pour into the simmering vegetables.
Mix well.

4. Season the vegetables with salt and pepper and serve with the pigs knuckles.

Pork Fillet (Tenderloin) with Peach Chutney

1. Wash the pork fillet and wipe dry. Cut it into slices 2.5 cm / 1 in thick and flatten with the palm of your hand. Season the fillets on both sides with salt and pepper. Heat the oil in a non-stick pan and fry the pieces briskly on both sides for 3 minutes each side. Remove from the pan and keep in a warm place.

2. For the chutney: Blanch the peaches, peel, remove the stones (pits) and dice. Put the peaches, vinegar, soy sauce and peach preserve in a saucepan and stir well. Simmer over medium heat for 5–7 minutes. The chutney should have a thick consistency.

3. Arrange the slices of pork fillet on two warmed plates and garnish with the chutney. Serve with rice.

Two servings

15 minutes

2 grilled pork knuckles from the butcher
250 g (generous half pound) tomatoes
500 g (1 generous pound) onions
3 tablespoons of oil
1 teaspoon flour
3 tablespoons heavy cream
salt
pepper

199

Asparagus Gratin with Parmesan

Four servings

15 minutes

500 g (18 oz) green asparagus
500 g (18 oz) white asparagus
salt
1 pinch sugar
200 g / 7 oz (1 generous cup) grated Parmesan
125 g / 4 1/2 oz (5/8 cup) herb butter

1. Wash the green asparagus, peel the white asparagus and remove the woody ends. Cook the asparagus in salted water with a pinch of sugar for about 10 minutes until done. Remove from the water and drain.

2. Put the asparagus in a greased gratin dish, sprinkle with Parmesan and dot with flakes of herb butter. Brown under the preheated grill for 3 minutes.

Tagliatelle with Green Asparagus and Chanterelles

1. Wash the asparagus, remove the woody ends, halve lengthways and cook gently in boiling water for about 5 minutes until cooked. Remove from the water, drain and keep warm in a pan on the stove with about 20 g / 3/4 oz (1 1/2 tablespoons) butter.

2. Cook the tagliatelle al dente in the asparagus stock . Cut the ham into strips.

3. Clean and wash the chanterelles, peel and chop the shallot. Remove the leaves from the sprig of thyme and braise the chanterelles, shallots and thyme lightly in the remaining butter for about 5–8 minutes.

4. Drain the tagliatelle and arrange in plates together with the asparagus and chanterelles. Put the ham on top and sprinkle with olive oil. Season with salt and pepper and sprinkle with Parmesan.

Four servings
15 minutes

1 kg (2 1/4 lb) green asparagus
salt
50 g (4 tablespoons) butter
250 g (9 oz) tagliatelle
4 slices smoked ham
250 g (9 oz) fresh chanterelles
1 shallot
1 sprig thyme
6 tablespoons olive oil
freshly ground pepper
125 g / 4 1/2 oz (1 1/4 cups) freshly grated or shaved Parmesan cheese

Zabaglione with Blackberries

Two servings

15 minutes

2 fresh egg yolks
2 tablespoons icing (con-
fectioner's) sugar
50 ml (3 tablespoons)
Marsala
1 teaspoon lemon juice
150 g / 5 oz (3/4 cup) fresh
blackberries

1. Put the egg yolks and icing (confectioner's) sugar in a pudding bowl and whisk with an electric hand-mixer for about 5 minutes on the highest speed until the mixture has become thick and creamy.

2. Add the Marsala and lemon juice. Heat some water in a large saucepan and keep warm over a low heat. Put the pudding bowl in the water, as a bain marie, and beat the creamy mixture until the mixture becomes very thick. Then place the bowl briefly in cold water to cool the mixture.

3. Wash the blackberries and arrange on two plates, pour the zabaglione on top and serve immediately.

1. Melt 3 tablespoons butter in a pan. Peel the onions, cut into thin rings and sauté until transparent.

2. Cut the smoked sausage into cubes, add to the onions and sauté also.

3. Peel the apples, remove the cores and quarter. Cut into thick slices. Melt the remaining butter in a saucepan and cook the apples gently. Add raisins, honey and spices.

4. Wash the marjoram, pluck off the leaves and chop finely. Place the apple mixture on a large platter, arrange the smoked sausage on top and sprinkle with marjoram.

Four servings
20 minutes

2 onions
4 tablespoons butter
300 g (10 oz) smoked sausage
400 g (14 oz) apples
3 tablespoons raisins
3 tablespoons honey
paprika
salt
freshly ground pepper
1 sprig marjoram

203
Chinese Cabbage-Mushroom Dish

Four servings

20 minutes

2 tablespoons oil
2 shallots, cut into thin rings
2 cloves garlic, pressed
1 teaspoon grated ginger
1 teaspoon honey
500 g (1 generous pound) champignons, cleaned and cut in half
500 g (1 generous pound) whole agaric mushrooms, cleaned
2 teaspoons soy sauce
basil
Basmati rice

1. Heat oil in a pan. Sauté the shallots and garlic and then add the champignons, ginger and honey. Stir vigorously and brown. Add in the agaric mushrooms and the soy sauce and stir carefully. Sprinkle with basil.

2. In the meantime prepare 4 cups of basmati rice according to the directions on the package and serve as a side dish.

1. Wash and prepare the celery and pepper. Remove the seeds from the pepper. Peel the onions. Rub the mushrooms clean with kitchen paper. Cut all the vegetables into thin strips.

2. Put the cornflour (corn starch) in a small bowl. Add the soy sauce, sherry and 1 tablespoon water, stir to obtain a smooth mixture and leave to stand briefly.

3. Heat the sesame oil in a wok or large pan. Add the vegetables and fry for about 5 minutes, stirring continuously. The vegetables must be cooked but still crisp.

4. Wash the bean sprouts, dab dry and add to the vegetables. Cook for another minute.

5. Stir the cornflour (corn starch) mixture briefly again and add slowly to the vegetables in the pan. Bring quickly to the boil, stirring continuously. Simmer for 2 more minutes over a low heat while stirring. Season with salt and pepper and serve immediately.

Two servings

20 minutes

1/2 stick (stalk) celery
1/2 red sweet pepper
1/2 onion
2 mushrooms
1 teaspoon cornflour (corn starch)
1 tablespoon soy sauce
2 teaspoons sherry
1 1/2 tablespoons sesame oil
100 g / 3 1/2 oz (2 cups) mung bean sprouts
75 g / 3 oz (1 1/2 cups) soya bean sprouts
salt
freshly ground pepper

205 Chop Suey (Variation)

Two servings
20 minutes

See recipe 204

Vary this dish as you like by adding small cut pieces of chicken, turkey—or, if you prefer seafood, crab meat or prawns.

Hearty Vegetable Dish 206

1. Dice the slices of salami and the onions. Peel the potatoes and cut in fine wedges. Cut the peppers in half, remove the seeds and cut in strips.
2. Heat oil in a frying pan and brown the salami and onions.
3. Add the potatoes and peppers, cover and let everything simmer over a low heat.
4. As soon as the vegetables are tender, fold in the previously beaten eggs. When they have thickened, the dish is ready to serve.
5. Sprinkle amply with freshly chopped parsley and place on the table.

Four servings
20 minutes

8 slices hard salami
2 onions
8 potatoes
6 green peppers
4 tablespoons ci
4 tomatoes
4 eggs
fresh parsley

Broad Beans in Bacon Sauce

1. Clean the potatoes thoroughly and cook until tender in a pressure cooker.

2. In the meantime, dice the bacon and heat in a pot so that the fat separates out. Add flour to the fat and stir until the mixture turns light yellow. Then pour in the milk while stirring continuously.

3. Pour the water into a pot, add a pinch of salt and cook the beans until soft. Drain.

4. Pour a little of the bean water into the bacon sauce until the sauce is smooth and then add the beans. Season with pepper, savoury and parsley and serve with the boiled potatoes.

Four servings

20 minutes

12 medium sized potatoes
80 g (scant 3 oz) smoked bacon
1–2 tablespoons flour
1/8 l (1/2 cup) milk
1/4 l (1 cup) water
salt
750 g (generous 1 1/2 pounds) fresh broad beans
pepper
savoury
fresh parsley

Far Eastern Vegetable Dish

Four servings

20 minutes

4 cups basmati rice
250 g / scant 9 oz (2 1/2 cups) French-sliced beans
250 g / scant 9 oz (2 1/2 cups) peas
125 g (generous 4 oz) cucumber, cut in strips
2 tablespoons butter
8 large shallots, diced
2 zucchini, sliced
spring onions
250 ml / 8 fl oz (1 cup) milk
125 ml / 4 fl oz (1/2 cup) water
1 tablespoon soy sauce
1 tablespoon honey
1 pinch chili flakes
1 tomato, remove the seeds and chop
1 fresh, red chilli pepper, diced
1 bunch of Italian parsley, chopped

1. Prepare basmati rice according to the directions on the packet.
2. In the meantime boil salted water in a pot and blanch the beans, peas, cucumber and zucchini for a minute. Take out and rinse under cold water.
3. Heat the butter in a deep pan and simmer the shallots until tender. Combine milk and water with the soy sauce, honey and chili flakes in the wok and bring to a boil quickly.
4. Add the vegetables with tomato and chili and simmer for 5 minutes. Garnish with freshly chopped parsley and serve with the rice.

Chinese Fried Vegetables with Smoked Tofu

1. Bring plenty of boiling water to the boil, add the buckwheat pasta and cook following the instructions on the packet. Peel the carrots, shallots and garlic. Cut the carrots into small cubes. Chop the onion and garlic finely. Clean the mushrooms and finely dice. Rinse the bean sprouts and drain the pasta.

2. Heat the sesame oil in a deep pan or wok and fry the shallots, garlic, carrots, mushrooms and bean sprouts for 5 minutes, stirring continuously. Cut the smoked tofu into cubes and add to the frying vegetables.

3. Fry briefly but briskly and season with soy sauce, lime juice, salt and pepper. Sprinkle with chopped coriander just before serving.

Two servings

20 minutes

sea salt
100 g (3 1/2 oz) buckwheat pasta
3 large carrots
2 shallots
1 clove garlic
120 g (4 oz) oyster mushrooms
3 tablespoons soy sauce
2 teaspoons sesame oil
100 g (3 1/2 oz) smoked tofu
soy sauce
1 teaspoon lime juice
freshly ground pepper
1 tablespoon chopped green coriander

210 Far Eastern Dish with Smoked Tofu (Variation)

Two servings

20 minutes

See recipe 209

This healthy, delicious dish can be varied at will by using different kinds of noodles and vegetables or rice noodles.

Fish and Cucumber 211

1. Peel and dice the potatoes, and cook in salted water until tender.

2. Sprinkle the fish with lemon juice and salt lightly.

3. Heat the butter in a pot and carefully add flour while stirring. Then stir in the cream.

4. Place the fish in the sauce and cook until done over very low heat. In the meantime, peel the cucumbers, slice thinly and add to the fish.

5. Season the dish with salt and pepper.

6. Arrange the fish on a platter with the potatoes and pour the sauce over both. Garnish with dill.

Four servings

20 minutes

6 large potatoes
800 g (1 3/4 pounds) fish fillet (for example red perch)
lemon juice
salt
3 tablespoons butter
3 tablespoons flour
250 g / 9 oz (1 cup) heavy cream
1 small cucumber
pepper
dill

Fish Fillets on a Bed of Rocket and Cucumber

1. Pre-heat the oven to 180 °C (350 °F), gas mark 4.

2. Drizzle lime juice and olive oil on the fish and sprinkle it with the oregano and thyme. Grill for about 7–10 minutes.

3. Wash and prepare the rocket, peel the cucumber and cut into thin slices. Arrange on two large plates.

4. Put the salt, pepper, thistle oil, vegetable stock and balsamic vinegar in a bowl and stir to make a smooth dressing. Pour over the salad. Divide the fish into portions and arrange on the salad.

Two servings
20 minutes

300 g (10 oz) fillets of fish (for instance cod)
1 tablespoon lime juice
1 tablespoon olive oil
1 teaspoon dried oregano
1 teaspoon dried thyme
100 g (3 1/2 oz) rocket
1 small cucumber
salt
freshly ground pepper
1 teaspoon thistle oil
1 tablespoon vegetable stock
1 tablespoon balsamic vinegar

Two servings

20 minutes

300 g (10 oz) pollack fillets
1 tablespoon lemon juice
1 teaspoon fresh lemon balm
freshly ground pepper
1 teaspoon sunflower oil
1 clove garlic
150 g (5 oz) fresh leaf spinach
sea salt
1 pinch grated nutmeg
100 g / 3 1/2 oz (3/8 cup) low-fat yoghurt (1.5%)
1 tablespoon chopped parsley
1 tablespoon pine kernels

1. Sprinkle the lemon juice over the fish and scatter the chopped lemon balm on top. Season with pepper. Heat the sunflower oil in a large non-stick pan and fry the fish for about 5 minutes. Shred into large pieces with two forks.

2. Peel the garlic and chop finely. Add to the braised fish and continue braising. Wash and sort out the spinach but do not dry. Put the wet spinach in the pan with the fish and braise for a few minutes until the leaves have become soft.

3. Season with salt and grated nutmeg. Stir in the yoghurt and simmer for a few minutes over a low heat. Sprinkle chopped parsley and pine kernels over the fish and spinach.

Chicken Livers in Tomato Sauce

214

1. Rinse the chicken livers and pat dry with kitchen paper. Peel the shallots and carrots and slice both finely. Peel the tomatoes, cut into quarters and remove the seeds. Cut the tomatoes into strips. Chop the thyme.

2. Heat 2 tablespoons oil in a pan, add the livers and fry. Season with salt and pepper. Put to one side.

3. Heat the remaining oil in a pan. Add the shallot rings and sliced carrots. Add the ketchup and stir well. Cook briefly. Add the tomatoes and herbs and simmer for about 10 minutes.

4. Heat up the chicken livers briefly and serve with the tomato sauce. Season again with salt and pepper just before serving.

Four servings
20 minutes

600 g (1 1/4 lb) chicken livers
3 shallots
2 carrots
500 g (18 oz) tomatoes
1/2 bunch thyme
4 tablespoons oil
salt
pepper
1 tablespoon tomato ketchup

Smoked Ribs
with Sauerkraut

Four servings
20 minutes

750 g (generous
1 1/2 pound) sauerkraut
1 tablespoon butter
2 onions
juniper berries
200 ml (3/4 cup) white wine
4 smoked rib pork chops
prepared by the butcher

1. Place a small portion of the sauerkraut in a
bowl, cover and set aside.
2. Melt the butter in a pot. Dice the onions
and place in a pot together with the larger
amount of sauerkraut. Add the juniper berries
and the white wine and simmer the sauerkraut
for about 15 minutes. Stir occasionally.
3. Before serving, combine the raw sauerkraut
with the cooked sauerkraut. Arrange the
sauerkraut on four plates around the ribs and
bring to the table.

Asparagus with Salmon Steak and Prawns (Shrimp)

1. Peel the asparagus and remove the woody ends. Cook the asparagus in boiling salted water for 20 minutes until done.

2. Season the salmon with salt and pepper, coat in flour and fry on each side for 3–4 minutes in butter. Add the prawns (shrimps) and heat again.

3. Heat the hollandaise sauce.

4. Remove the asparagus from the water, drain and arrange on the plates with the salmon and prawns (shrimps). Pour the sauce on top.

Four servings
20 minutes

1.5 kg (3 lb) white asparagus
salt
4 salmon steaks (about 150 g; 5 1/2 oz each)
freshly ground pepper
2 tablespoons flour
40 g (3 tablespoons) butter
200 g (7 oz) prawns (shrimps)
250 ml (1 cup) hollandaise sauce (packet mix)

217 Giant Prawn Kebabs

Four servings

20 minutes

8 ripe beef tomatoes
3 tablespoons olive oil
1 teaspoon dried Italian
herbs
salt
1 pinch sugar
lemon pepper
24 large prawns (shrimps),
without head and peeled
60 g (4 tablespoons)
clarified butter

1. Peel the tomatoes, cut into quarters and remove the seeds. Cut the tomato pieces into small cubes. Heat the olive oil in a pan, add the diced tomatoes and cook until the mixture thickens, stirring all the time. Season with herbs, salt, sugar and pepper. Put the sauce in a warm place.

2. Thread the prawns (shrimps) on four wooden skewers. Heat the clarified butter in a large pan and fry the skewers on both sides for about 5 minutes over a medium heat.

3. Pour the tomato sauce on the plates and arrange the prawns (shrimps) on top. Sprinkle with salt and pepper.

Veal Escalope with Tomato and Olive Purée

1. Drain the tomatoes and mozzarella. Cut the cheese into four slices. Put the tomatoes in the liquidizer and purée at the highest speed. Chop the olives and add to the tomato purée with the pressed garlic. Add a little sugar and season generously with salt and pepper.

2. Beat the escalopes lightly and sprinkle with a little salt. Heat the oil in a very large pan and add the veal escalopes. Cover them completely with tomato purée and sprinkle with oregano.

3. As soon as the escalopes are cooked, cover each with a slice of mozzarella. Cover the pan. The escalopes are ready to be served as soon as the mozzarella begins to melt.

Four servings

20 minutes

1 pack mozzarella cheese (200 g; 7 oz)
1 large can tomatoes (800 g; 1 3/4 lb)
16 black olives, stoned (pitted)
1 clove garlic
salt
sugar
pepper
4 escalopes of veal
6 tablespoons olive oil
1/2 teaspoon chopped oregano

Egg Fricassée with Asparagus

Four servings

20 minutes

500 g (18 oz) green
asparagus
salt
1 pinch sugar
8 eggs
250 ml / 8 fl oz (1 cup) milk
250 ml / 8 fl oz (1 cup) cream
50 g (4 tablespoons) butter
80 g (3 oz) porridge (rolled)
oats
freshly ground pepper
juice of 1/2 lemon
1 bunch parsley

1. Wash the asparagus thoroughly, removing the woody ends. Cut the asparagus into pieces of 3 cm / 1 1/4 in length and cook in salted water with a pinch of sugar for about 10 minutes until done. Remove from the water and drain.

2. Hard-boil (hard-cook) the eggs, shell and cut in slices with an egg-slicer.

3. Mix 250 ml / 8 fl oz (1 cup) asparagus stock , milk and cream and bring to the boil together with the butter. Stir the Porridge (rolled) oats into a small amount of asparagus stock , add to the milk and cream mixture, and bring back to the boil.

4. Add the asparagus and eggs to the sauce and heat up slowly over a low heat. Leave to infuse. Season with salt, pepper and lemon juice and garnish with finely chopped parsley.

Pork Chops with Apple Cream

1. Peel the apples, remove the cores and quarter. Cut into thin slices.

2. Melt 2 tablespoons of butter in a pan. Add the apple slices and sauté while stirring. Pour in with wine and add the cinnamon.

3. In a second pan, melt the remaining butter. Wash the pork chops and season with salt and pepper. Brown them quickly in the butter over a high heat, turning once. Reduce the heat and cook gently until done.

4. Mix the crème fraîche with the apple mixture. Allow to cook until the apples disintegrate and season with pepper, salt and lemon juice. Serve with the pork chops in a separate dish.

Four servings

20 minutes

250 g (1/2 lb) apples
4 tablespoons butter
125 ml / 4 fl oz (1/2 cup) dry white wine
sprinkling of cinnamon
8 pork chops
salt
freshly ground white pepper
8 tablespoons crème fraîche
1 to 2 tablespoons green pepper
1 teaspoon lemon juice

221

Asparagus with Saffron and Hollandaise Sauce

Four servings
20 minutes

1 kg (2 1/4 lb) green asparagus
1 kg (2 1/4 lb) white asparagus
salt
1 pinch sugar
10 g (2 teaspoons) butter

For the hollandaise sauce:
1 pinch of saffron threads
2 teaspoons lemon juice
salt
freshly ground pepper
3 egg yolks
200 g (1 cup) butter
25 g (1/4 cup) flaked (slivered) almonds

1. Wash the green asparagus, peel the white asparagus and remove the woody ends. Cook the white asparagus for about 10 minutes and the green asparagus for about 8 minutes in gently simmering salted water together with sugar and butter.

2. To make the hollandaise sauce: dissolve the saffron in 4 teaspoons hot water, add the lemon juice, salt, pepper and egg yolks and stir until the mixture is smooth. Whisk over a bain-marie until foamy. Gradually add the lumps of butter and finally the lightly roasted almonds.

3. Remove the asparagus from the stock, drain and serve with the hollandaise sauce.

Apple Dumplings

1. Melt the butter in a small pan. Mix the flour, eggs, salt and milk or water in a bowl. Add the melted butter and stir with a wooden spoon until the dough pulls away from the sides of the bowl.

2. Peel, quarter and core the apples. Cut into very small pieces or grate them. Add to the dough and stir in carefully.

3. Bring a large saucepan of salted water to the boil. With a spoon, scoop out the dough into little dumplings and slide immediately into the boiling water. Do not have too many in the water at once.

4. Cook the dumplings for about 10 minutes. Remove from the water with a slotted spoon and drain well. Arrange on plates and garnish with butter, sugar and cinnamon.

Four servings
20 minutes

1 tablespoon butter
500 g (4 1/2 cups) flour
2 eggs
salt
125 ml (1/2 cup) milk or water
500 g (1 lb) apples
butter for serving
sugar
cinnamon

Squid Rings in a Tomato Cream Sauce

Four servings

20 minutes

800 g (1 3/4 lb) squid rings, frozen
juice of 1 lemon
1/2 bunch chervil
5 beef tomatoes
250 ml (1 cup) white wine
2 tablespoons oil
salt
lemon pepper
1 tablespoon crème fraîche

1. Defrost the squid rings, rinse and wipe dry with kitchen paper. Sprinkle with lemon juice. Chop the chervil.
2. Peel the tomatoes, cut into quarters and remove the seeds. Chop the tomato pieces finely and purée in the liquidizer on high speed.
3. Heat the oil in a pan, fry the squid and season with salt and pepper. Remove from the pan. Add the tomato purée and crème fraîche to the pan, bring to the boil gently and season with salt and pepper. Arrange the rings on a dish with the tomato and cream sauce and sprinkle with chervil just before serving.

Tomato and Goat's Cheese Bread Gratin

1. Slice the tomatoes and goat's cheese. Sprinkle herb salt and a little freshly ground pepper on the tomato slices. Cut the baguette diagonally into 12 slices.

2. Pre-heat the oven to 200 °C (400 °F), gas mark 6. Heat 4 tablespoons of olive oil in a pan. Fry the baguette slices briefly on both sides and leave to cool slightly.

3. Grease a gratin dish with 1 tablespoon of oil. Arrange the slices of bread, tomatoes and cheese in alternate layers in the gratin dish. Pour the rest of the olive oil over the gratin. Bake in the oven for about 10 minutes.

4. Shortly before the gratin is ready, sprinkle with walnuts and basil. Serve hot.

Four servings
20 minutes

5 large tomatoes
200 g (7 oz) goat's cheese
herb salt
freshly ground pepper
1/2 baguette
7 tablespoons olive oil
35 g (3/8 cup) coarsely chopped walnut kernels
1 small bunch basil, finely chopped

East-West Mushroom Pancake

Four servings

20 minutes

2 tablespoons thistle oil
4 onions, sliced in rings
1 chili pepper, sliced in thin rings
20 fresh shitake mushrooms; remove the stems and slice the caps.
1 packet mungo bean sprouts
8 shallots, cut in small pieces
1 tablespoon fish sauce
4 large, very thin pancakes (see recipe number 54—but without sugar; make them fresh and keep them warm)
1 teaspoon ground curkuma
basil
green coriander
chili sauce

1. Heat the oil in the frying pan and sauté the onions until golden. Remove the onions and mix them with the chili peppers. Set aside.

2. Reheat the pan (if necessary, add more oil) and brown the mushrooms, bean sprouts, shallots and fish sauce for several minutes, until the mixture is well done.

3. Place the pancakes on 4 pre-warmed plates and sprinkle with curkuma. Spoon the chili and onions into the middle of the pancakes and top with the mushroom-bean sprout mixture. Then fold the pancake in half

4. Sprinkle the folded pancakes with basil and green coriander and serve with chili sauce as dip.

Wiener Schnitzel with French Fries

1. Distribute the French fries on a baking sheet and bake in a pre-heated oven according to the directions on the packet.

2. In the meantime rinse the veal escalopes and pat dry. beat them thin. Combine the flour with a bit of salt and pepper on a flat plate. Beat 4 eggs in a shallow bowl.

3. Draw the veal through the flour and then through the beaten eggs. Finally dip both sides into the breading flour.

4. Heat the butter in a pan and fry the veal for about 2 minutes on each side.

5. Place the schnitzel and French fries on 4 plates. Quarter the lemon and place one slice on each plate before serving.

Four servings
20 minutes

600 g (generous
1 1/2 pound) french fries
(frozen)
4 escalopes of veal
2 eggs
5 tablespoons flour
salt
pepper
200 g (1 generous cup) flour
for breading
2 tablespoons butter
1 lemon

227

Variation: Wiener schnitzel can also be garnished with capers and olives.

Sausage Gulasch

Two servings

20 minutes

4 knackwurst or similar
sausages
4 carrots
2 tomatoes
1 onion
3 tablespoons of butter
1/2 l/ 17 fl oz (2 cups) stock
salt
flour
2 pickles
rose paprika

1. Cut the sausages in slices. Dice the carrots, tomatoes and onion.

2. Melt half the butter in a pan and brown the diced ingredients.

3. After several minutes, pour in the stock and season the mixture with salt. Cover and let simmer.

4. In the meantime draw the sausage slices through flour and fry in a second pan in the remaining butter. Dice the pickles.

5. Add the fried sausage slices and the diced pickles to the pan with the vegetables. Let them steep a moment. Season with salt and rose paprika and serve.

Zander Fillet with Rice, Plums and Fennel

1. Cook the rice in salted water following the instructions on the packet. Wash and prepare the fennel, then cut into thin strips. Peel the shallots and ginger and chop finely. Rub the plums clean with kitchen paper, remove the stones and cut into small pieces.

2. Rinse the zander fillet, wipe dry, cut into bite-sized pieces and sprinkle with the juice of 1/2 a lime.

3. Heat the oil in a pan and fry the zander fillet on both sides in the hot oil. Season with salt and pepper. Add the fennel, shallots, ginger and plums and cook for about 6 minutes. Season with the rest of the lime juice, salt, pepper, honey and soy sauce.

4. Arrange the zander fillet with the plums and fennel on two warmed dishes and serve with basmati rice.

Two servings
20 minutes

100 g / 3 1/2 oz (5/8 cups) basmati rice
sea salt
1 bulb fennel
2 shallots
1 piece fresh ginger (about 3 cm; 1 1/4 in long)
120 g (4 oz) plums
400 g (14 oz) zander fillets
juice of 1 lime
2 teaspoons cooking oil
freshly ground pepper
1 teaspoon acacia honey
soy sauce

230

Asparagus and Chicken Breast Vol-au-Vents

Four servings

25 minutes

150 g / 5 1/2 oz (1 cup) peas
2 spring onions (scallions)
60 g / 2 oz (1/4 cup) sugar
1 kg (2 1/4 lb) white asparagus
25 g (2 tablespoons) butter
salt
1 pinch sugar
400 g (14 oz) chicken breast fillets
1 tablespoon curry powder
1 tablespoon flour
200 ml / 7 fl oz (7/8 cup) chicken stock , made from a cube
4 tablespoons cream
20 g (3/4 oz) capers with liquid
1 tablespoon lemon juice
freshly ground white pepper
4 large puff pastry vol-au-vent cases

1. Wash and prepare the peas and spring onions (scallions). Cut the spring onions (scallions) into rings. Wash the peas. Peel the asparagus, remove the woody ends and cut into small pieces.

2. Melt the butter and fry the onions, peas and asparagus for 5 minutes. Season with salt and pepper. Cut the chicken into cubes, add to the pan and fry lightly. Sprinkle curry powder and flour over the meat and other ingredients and stir well. Next add the chicken stock and cream, stirring constantly. Cover and simmer for 5 minutes. Stir in the peas and capers with their juice. Season with lemon juice and pepper. Simmer gently for another 5 minutes.

3. Arrange the vol-au-vents on the plates and fill with the asparagus and chicken mixture.

Green Asparagus with Rolled Sole

1. Wash the asparagus, remove the woody ends and cook in gently simmering salted water for 8–10 minutes until done.

2. Place the slices of pork loin on the smooth side of the sole fillets, roll up and secure. Bring the salted water and lemon juice to the boil, add the rolled sole and pork and simmer for 12 minutes.

3. Heat up the hollandaise sauce. Remove the asparagus and rolled sole and pork from the water and drain. Arrange on plates and pour the hollandaise sauce on top.

Four servings
25 minutes

1.5 kg (3 lb) green asparagus
salt
8 slices smoked cured loin
of pork
8 fillets of sole (about 100 g;
3 1/2 oz each)
juice of 1 lemon
250 ml (1 cup) hollandaise
sauce (packet mix)

Chicory with Polenta

Four servings

25 minutes

3/4 l (3 cups) beef or
vegetable stock
200 g (1 1/4 cups) polenta
(cornmeal)
500 g (1 generous pound)
chicory
1 tablespoon butter
1/4 l (1 cup) water
salt
2 tablespoons butter for
browning

1. Bring the stock to a boil and stir in the cornmeal with a whisk. Let it simmer at low heat for about 5 minutes. Remove from the stove and let rest for 10 minutes to absorb the liquid.

2. Remove any damaged leaves from the chicory. Briefly wash the remaining leaves.

3. Bring the water and the butter to a boil. Place the chicory in the water, add a bit of salt and boil until tender.

4. In the meantime brown 2 tablespoons of butter in a saucepan.

5. Place the chicory on a plate, pour on the browned butter and serve with the polenta.

Chicken Breasts with Hollandaise Sauce

1. Wash the chicken fillets, wipe them dry and season with herb salt and pepper. Heat the butter in a small pan and fry the chicken breasts for 6 minutes on each side until golden brown.

2. Peel and dice the carrots. Clean, wash and prepare the leeks and cut into rings. Peel and dice the potatoes. Cook the vegetables in a little salted water for about 15 minutes until tender.

3. Dice half the smoked salmon into small cubes and make small rosettes from the remaining salmon. Warm the Hollandaise sauce over a low heat, stirring continuously.

4. Arrange the finely diced salmon in the middle of two plates. Put the chicken breasts with the Hollandaise sauce on top with the vegetables next to them. Garnish with the salmon rosettes, parsley and salmon roe. Serve immediately.

Two servings

25 minutes

2 halved chicken breast fillets
herb salt
freshly ground pepper
1 tablespoon butter
2 carrots
1 leek
150 g (5 oz) waxy potatoes
80 g (3 oz) smoked fish
200 ml (7/8 cup) Hollandaise sauce
curly-leaved parsley
1 teaspoon salmon roe

Veal Medallions
with Asparagus

Four servings

25 minutes

500 g (18 oz) white
asparagus
750 g (1 1/2 lb) green
asparagus
salt
1 teaspoon sugar
juice of 1/2 lemon
8 medallions of veal (about
80 g; 3 oz each)
freshly ground pepper
20 g (1 1/2 tablespoons)
clarified butter
100 ml / 3 1/2 fl oz (scant
1/2 cup) dry white wine
2 tablespoons wheat flour
100 ml / 3 1/2 fl oz (scant
1/2 cup) meat stock
100 ml / 3 1/2 fl oz (scant
1/2 cup) cream
1 1/2 tablespoons butter

1. Peel the white asparagus, wash the green asparagus and remove the woody ends. Cook the white asparagus for 15 minutes and the green asparagus for 10 minutes in gently simmering salted water with sugar and lemon juice.

2. Season the veal medallions with salt and pepper and fry in clarified butter for 3 minutes on each side. Remove from the pan and keep in a warm place.

3. Deglaze the cooking juices with wine. Stir in the flour and meat stock , stirring constantly, and reduce a little. Add the cream and season with salt and pepper.

4. Remove the asparagus from the stock, drain and toss in hot butter.

Käsespätzle
(Cheese Noodles)

1. Bring a pot of salted water to boil. Cook the spätzle in the water according to the directions on the package. Drain. In the meantime grate the Emmental and Appenzell cheeses and mix them together. Pre-heat the oven to 150 °C (300 °F), gas mark 2.

2. Cover the bottom of a heatproof casserole with a layer of spätzle. Cover the spätzle with an ample layer of cheese. Then add another layer of spätzle, and so on. Bake the spätzle in the oven for 10 minutes.

3. In the meantime, heat the butter in a skillet and sauté the onions until brown. Distribute the onions over the spätzle.

Serve with potato salad or lettuce.

Four servings

25 minutes

500 g (1 generous pound) spätzle or noodles (from the packet)
200 g (7 oz) Emmental cheese
100 g (scant 4 oz) Appenzell cheese
2 tablespoons butter
2 large onions, diced

Asparagus Gratin

Four servings
25 minutes

2 kg (4 1/2 lb) white asparagus
salt
1 pinch sugar
butter
3 tomatoes
2 onion
2–3 tablespoons finely chopped basil
freshly ground pepper
150 g (5 1/2 oz) Gorgonzola
3 tablespoons crème fraîche

1. Peel the asparagus, remove the woody ends. Cook the asparagus in salted water with a pinch of sugar and a little butter for 10 minutes until done. Remove the asparagus from the water, drain and put in a well buttered gratin dish.

2. Blanch the tomatoes, skin and chop up. Peel the onion, chop finely and braise lightly in the hot butter together with the chopped tomatoes. Add the basil, season with salt and pepper and pour the sauce over the asparagus.

3. Cut the cheese into small cubes, stir into the crème fraîche and pour over the tomatoes and asparagus. Brown under the pre-heated oven grill for about 5 minutes.

1. Heat 2 tablespoons of the oil in the pan together with 1 chopped clove garlic and brown. Add the meat and chilli peppers and sauté quickly over a high flame until the meat is brown and crispy on the outside.

2. Combine the remaining garlic with the fish sauce, honey, a little salt and a tablespoon of oil in a bowl together with the meat. Mix well. Leave to marinate for about 15 minutes.

3. In another bowl, place the chopped onion and vinegar. Season with sesame oil, salt and pepper. Arrange the onion mixture on a platter with the meat and sprinkle with the marinade.

4. Serve with fresh leaves of lettuce, rice, vegetables and seafood.

Four servings

25 minutes

3 tablespoons oil
5 cloves garlic, chopped
500 g (1 generous pound) beef steak, diced
4 chili peppers, finely cut
1 tablespoon fish sauce
1 teaspoon honey
1 onion, finely cut
1 teaspoon sesame oil
salt
pepper
1 tablespoon vinegar

Noodles with Ham

Four servings
25 minutes

200 g (7 oz) spaghetti
3 tablespoons butter
1 clove garlic, pressed
100 g (scant 4 oz) cooked ham
200 g (3/4 cup) heavy cream
salt
black pepper
oregano
30 g (1 oz) grated pecorino cheese

1. Bring a pot of salted water to boil. Add the spaghetti and cook according to the directions on the packet. Strain off the water.

2. Heat the butter in a pan and add the garlic and thinly cut strips of ham. Sauté for about two minutes. Add the spaghetti and stir well. Sauté the mixture for another 3–5 minutes.

3. Combine salt, pepper, oregano and pecorino with the cream. Pour the sauce over the spaghetti and let it simmer over low heat for another 3–5 minutes. Garnish with basil leaves and serve.

239

Variation for vegetarians:
Instead of cooked ham, use the same amount of smoked tofu.

Pork Medallions with Asparagus and Dill

1. Peel and chop the onions. Peel the asparagus, remove the woody ends and cut into pieces of 1 cm / 3/8 in length. Wash and dry the dill, and chop it finely. Rinse the medallions in cold water and season with salt and pepper.

2. Heat 80 g / 3 oz (6 tablespoons) butter and oil in a pan and fry the meat for 2–3 minutes on both sides. Remove from the pan and keep warm in the oven at the lowest setting, 80 °C (180 °F).

3. Sweat the onion and asparagus in the cooking fat, add the veal stock and lemon juice and simmer for 7 minutes. Stir the remaining butter, a little at a time, into the sauce. Reduce a little and stir in the dill.

4. Arrange the medallions on the plates, pour the asparagus sauce on top and garnish with crabmeat.

Four servings

25 minutes

4 onions
800 g (1 3/4 lb) white asparagus
2 bunches dill
12 pork medallions (about 800 g; 1 3/4 lb)
salt
freshly ground pepper
250 g (1 1/4 cups) ice-cold butter
4 tablespoons oil
600 ml (2 1/2 cups) veal stock
4 tablespoons lemon juice
100 g (3 1/2 oz) crab meat

241

Tomato and Mozzarella Gratin

Four servings

25 minutes

2 packs mozzarella (200 g;
7 oz each)
800 g (1 3/4 lb) medium
sized tomatoes
1 clove garlic
1/2 bunch basil
1/2 bunch flat leaf parsley
3 slices crispbread
60 g (4 tablespoons) herb
butter
butter for the mould
salt
pepper
1/2 teaspoon dried Italian
herbs

1. Drain the mozzarella and slice. Cut the tomatoes into slices. Peel the clove of garlic and chop finely. Coarsely chop the basil and parsley.

2. Break the crispbread into small pieces, put in a liquidizer and turn into crumbs. Work the herb butter (at room temperature) into the bread crumbs.

3. Pre-heat the oven to 200 °C (400 °F), gas mark 6. Butter a gratin dish generously.

4. Arrange a layer of overlapping slices of tomatoes at the bottom and season with salt, pepper, garlic and herbs; follow by a layer of mozzarella; season with salt and pepper. Continue until all the tomatoes and mozzarella have been used up. Finish off the gratin with a layer of the bread crumb and herb butter mixture.

5. Bake the gratin in the oven for about 15 minutes.

Zander with Braised Carrots and Mushrooms

1. Clean the mushrooms, rub them with kitchen paper and cut into slices. Peel the onions and garlic and chop finely. Peel the carrots and cut into thin strips.

2. Heat the vegetable stock in a large saucepan. Add the mushrooms and vegetables. Cover and braise for about 10–15 minutes. Add the crème fraîche and season with salt, pepper and grated nutmeg.

3. Sprinkle the zander fillets with lemon juice and place them in a non-stick pan. Pour in the white wine, cover and cook for 10 minutes. Arrange the braised vegetables and fish fillets on two plates and sprinkle with parsley.

Two servings
25 minutes

200 g (7 oz) mushrooms
2 onions
1 clove garlic
4 carrots
125 ml (1/2 cup) vegetable stock
1 tablespoon crème fraîche
salt
freshly ground pepper
grated nutmeg
2 zander fillets
1 tablespoon lemon juice
100 ml (1/2 cup) white wine
1 tablespoon chopped parsley

Curry Risotto with Apple

Four servings
30 minutes

20 g (3/4 oz) margarine
2 onions
250 g (8 oz) risotto rice
2 tablespoons curry powder
500 ml (2 1/4 cups) stock
500 g (1 lb) apples
2 tablespoons lemon juice
100 ml (scant 1/2 cup)
orange juice
1 bunch chervil

1. Melt the margarine in a saucepan. Peel the onions, cut into rings and sweat in the margarine until transparent.
2. Add the rice to the onions and stir until coated. Sauté. Sprinkle the curry powder over, pour in the stock and let everything simmer with the lid on for 15 minutes.
3. Wash the apples, remove the cores and quarter. Cut the quarters into julienne sticks and put in a bowl. Pour over the lemon and orange juice and stir. Add the apples to the rice and cook over a gentle heat for 5–6 minutes.
4. Wash the chervil, pluck off the leaves and chop finely. Serve the curry risotto on plates garnished with the chopped chervil.

Sweet Pancakes (Crèpes) with Apples

1. Separate the eggs. In a bowl, mix the flour with the egg yolks, 1 tablespoon of sugar and the milk and stir until smooth. Beat the egg whites stiffly and fold into the batter. Stir carefully.

2. Peel, quarter and core the apples. Cut into small pieces. Add the rest of the sugar, the lemon peel and the rum and mix together carefully.

3. Add the apples to the bowl of batter and mix thoroughly.

4. Melt two tablespoons of butter in a large frying pan. Pour in the batter until the bottom of the pan is thickly covered. Brown the bottom of the pancake (crèpe) slowly over a low to medium heat. Turn and brown the other side.

5. In the pan, pull the pancake (crèpe) into pieces with two forks and brown the pieces on all sides while stirring constantly. Remove from the pan and keep warm. Repeat steps 4 and 5 until all the batter has been used up.

6. Arrange the pancake (crèpe) pieces on a platter and sprinkle with the coarse sugar and cinnamon.

Four servings

30 minutes

2 to 3 eggs
125 g (1 1/4 cups) plain (all purpose) flour
2 tablespoons sugar
125 ml (1/2 cup) milk
750 g (1 1/2 lb) apples
peel from 1 untreated lemon
1 tablespooon rum
100 g (1/2 cup) butter
coarse sugar
cinnamon

Bean and Apple Hot-pot with Smoked Pork

Four servings

10 minutes

100 g (3 1/2 oz) streaky bacon
500 g (1 lb) smoked loin of pork
2 onions
500 g (1 lb) green (snap) beans
20 g (1 1/2 tablespoons) butter
1 clove garlic
1 teaspoon dried savory
freshly ground pepper
125 ml (1/2 cup) apple juice
250 ml (1 cup) vegetable stock
400 g (14 oz) untreated apples

1. Dice the bacon and cut the smoked meat into large cubes. Peel the onions and cut into fine rings. Wash the beans and top and tail them.

2. Heat the butter in a large pan. Brown the bacon and meat evenly, add the onions and brown briefly together.

3. Peel and crush the garlic. Add the beans, savory, pepper and garlic to the meat. Pour in the apple juice and the vegetable stock Cook everything gently for 10 minutes over a medium heat.

4. Wash the apples thoroughly, remove the cores and quarter. Cut them into slices Add the apple slices to the pan with the meat and cook for a further 10 minutes. Check seasoning again before serving.

1. Wash and seperate the broccoli florets. Cook in lightly salted boiling water until tender.

2. Wash the sea trout, wipe dry and cook in gently simmering salted water with lemon juice for about 10 minutes until done. Divide into porticns and put aside in a warm place.

3. Grate the zest of an orange and squeeze to obtain the juice. Bring the orange juice to the boil with 125 ml / 4 fl oz (1 cup) water, stir in the hollandaise sauce mix and bring to the boil again. Stir flakes of butter, little by little, into the sauce. Add the orange zest and season with the salt and orange pepper.

4. Arrange the drained broccoli on four plates with the fish and pour the hollandaise on top. Garnish with slices of orange, dill and dill flowers.

Four servings
30 minutes

1 kg (2 1/4 lb) Broccoli
salt
2 salmon trout (about 400 g; 14 oz each)
4 tablespoons lemon juice
2 untreated oranges
30 g (1 oz) hollandaise sauce mix
125 g (5/8 cups) butter
ground orange pepper
1 bunch dill
dill umbels for garnish

Turkey Fricassée with Fennel

Four servings

30 minutes

800 g (1 3/4 lb) fennel
salt
sugar
80 g (6 teaspoons) butter
100 g (3 1/2 oz) button
mushrooms, canned or pre-
served in a jar
400 g (14 oz) turkey breast
2 tablespoons oil
225 ml (1 cup) cream
200 g (7 oz) mixed veg-
etable
freshly ground pepper
8 tablespoons breadcrumbs

1. Top and tail the fennel and wash . Slice into strips and cook until tender in lightly salted water.

2. Remove the button mushrooms from the jar or tin, drain and reserve 200 ml / 7 fl oz (7/8 cup) of the liquid. Cut the turkey meat into strips, fry in hot oil and take out of the pan. Add the mushroom liquid and cream to the cooking juices and bring to the boil to reduce and thicken.

3. Heat the meat, button mushrooms and mixed vegetables in the sauce and season with salt and pepper.

4. Heat the rest of the butter and fry the breadcrumbs in it. Arrange the fennel strips and turkey sauce on a plate and sprinkle with the fried breadcrumbs.

1. Peel the garlic and chop finely. Heat the olive oil in a large non-stick pan and fry the garlic in it.

2. Wash the rice and add to the pan. Fry for a few minutes, stirring all the time. Pour the vegetable stock into the pan with the garlic and rice. Season with salt and pepper.

3. Wash and prepare the Swiss chard and cut into strips 2 cm / 3/4 in wide. Add the Swiss chard to the rice in the pan. Cover and cook for about 10 minutes. Add more vegetable stock if necessary.

4. After about 10 minutes, put the fish fillets on top of the rice and Swiss chard mixture. Sprinkle with lemon juice. Cover and cook for a further 5–10 minutes until the fish is cooked.

5. Wash and dry the parsley, and chop the leaves finely. Arrange the rice and Swiss chard on two plates with the fish and sprinkle with the chopped parsley.

Two servings

30 minutes

1 clove garlic
1 tablespoon olive oil
120 g (4 oz) easy-cook rice
250 ml (1 cup) vegetable stock
salt
freshly ground pepper
250 g (9 oz) Swiss chard
300 g (10 oz) cod or pollack fillets
juice of 1 lemon
1/2 bunch parsley

Fish and Lime Couscous

Two servings
30 minutes

300 ml (1 1/4 cups) vegetable stock
1/2 teaspoon curry powder
100 g (3 1/2 oz) couscous
300 g (10 oz) rosefish
1 teaspoon groundnut oil
zest and juice of 2 untreated limes
1 pinch turmeric
1 pinch chilli pepper
2 tablespoons coconut milk
1/2 bunch fresh coriander

1. Heat the vegetable stock in a large pan and add the curry and couscous. Cover and cook over a low heat following the instructions on the packet. Add more liquid if necessary.
2. Cut the rosefish into broad strips. Heat the oil in a non-stick pan, add the fish and fry. Add the lime juice, lime zest, turmeric, chilli powder and coconut milk and bring to the boil again very briefly.
3. Carefully mix the fish and lime sauce with the couscous. Wash and dry the coriander, chop the leaves finely and sprinkle over the couscous.

Smoked Trout Fillets with Potatoes

1. Peel , quarter, and finally cook the potatoes in boiling salted water with butter for 20 minutes (they should remaining al dente however).

2. Mix the quark, crème fraîche, oil and two-thirds of the cress and liquidize in a blender until the mixture acquires a creamy texture. Add the remaining cress to this sauce and season with salt, pepper and lemon juice.

3. Remove the potatoes from the water, drain and arrange on the plates with the trout fillets. Pour the cress sauce on top or serve separately.

Four servings
30 minutes

1 kg (2 lb) potatoes
salt
1 teaspoon butter
1 pinch sugar
125 g (4 1/2 oz) quark
3 tablespoons crème fraîche
1 teaspoon oil
1 small box cress
freshly ground white pepper
2 tablespoons lemon juice
4 smoked trout fillets (about 150 g; 5 1/2 oz each)

251

Vegetable Kebabs with a Spicy Dip

Two servings

30 minutes

2 onions
2 small courgettes (zucchini)
75 g (3 oz) small mushrooms
1 red sweet pepper
125 ml (1/2 cup) vegetable stock
2 teaspoons groundnut oil
freshly ground pepper
juice of 1 lemon
2 metal or wooden skewers

for the dip:
5 tablespoons tomato ketchup (catsup)
1 tablespoon low-fat salad cream
1 clove garlic
1 pinch chilli pepper
1/2 bunch coriander

1. Peel and halve the onions. Wash and prepare the courgettes (zucchini) and cut into slices 2 cm / 3/4 in thick. Cut the woody ends off the mushrooms and rub clean with kitchen paper. Cut the pepper into four pieces, remove the stalk and seeds and cut into strips 2 cm / 3/4 in wide.
2. Heat the vegetable stock in a large saucepan, add the vegetables, cover and cook over medium heat for about 10 minutes.
3. Pre-heat the oven to 180 °C (350 °F), gas mark 4.
4. Remove the vegetables from the saucepan and drain well. Thread the onion halves, slices of courgette, strips of pepper and whole mushrooms in rotation on long metal or wooden skewers. Brush with oil. Grill for 10–15 minutes. Season with freshly ground pepper and sprinkle with lemon juice.
5. For the dip, mix the tomato ketchup (catsup) and salad cream together. Peel the garlic, chop finely. Wash and dry the coriander, and chop the leaves finely. Stir into the sauce. Season the dip with chilli powder and serve with the kebabs.

1. Wash the asparagus and remove the woody ends. Cook the asparagus in gently simmering salted water for 5 minutes until done. Remove from the water, rinse under cold water, drain and cut into pieces.

2. Wash the mangetouts (snow peas), peel and slice the carrots and blanch both in boiling salted water for 2 minutes. Remove from the water, rinse under cold water and drain.

3. Wash the courgettes (zucchini), cut off the stalks (stems), cut in half lengthways and slice thinly and sprinkle a little salt on top. Wash the chilli pepper, cut open lengthways and remove the stalk and white membrane from the inside. Cut into thin rings.

4. Fry the carrots and asparagus in 2 table-spoons soya oil for 2–3 minutes, then add the crushed garlic, chilli, courgettes (zucchini), mangetouts (snow peas) and crab. Season with soya sauce and pepper and garnish with finely chopped chervil.

Four servings

30 minutes

750 g (1 1/2 lb) asparagus
salt
150 g (5 1/2 oz) mangetouts (snow peas)
175 g (6 oz) carrots
3 small courgettes (zucchini)
1 chilli pod
2 tablespoons soya oil
2 clove garlic
300 g (11 oz) crab meat
3 tablespoons soya sauce
freshly ground pepper
1 bunch chervil

Spelt Grain Risotto

Two servings

30 minutes

150 g (5 oz) dried unripe
spelt grains
2 shallots
4 carrots
1 chilli pepper
1 teaspoon olive oil
400 ml (1 3/4 cups)
vegetable stock
1 bunch parsley
grated zest of 1 untreated
lemon
freshly ground pepper
sea salt

1. Soak the spelt grains overnight in a bowl of water.

2. Drain the spelt grains thoroughly. Peel the shallots and chop finely. Peel the carrots and cut into thin sticks. Wash and prepare the chillies, cut lengthways, remove the seeds and cut into fine strips.

3. Heat the olive oil in a large pan and fry the shallots until transparent. Add the spelt grains and fry briefly while stirring. Add the vegetable stock, carrots and chilli. Cover and simmer over a low heat for about 10–15 minutes.

4. Because the spelt swells up as it absorbs the liquid, it may be necessary to add more liquid. If there is too much liquid left at the end, it can be reduced by boiling it briskly over a high heat without a lid.

5. Wash and dry the parsley, chop the leaves finely and add to the pan. Season the spelt risotto with freshly ground pepper, salt and lemon zest.

1. Peel and dice the potatoes. Wash and clean the courgette and then slice. Peel the onion and the garlic and chop coarsely. Wash the oregano and thyme, pat dry and chop the leaves finely.

2. Heat vegetable stock in a flat casserole. Add the vegetables and herbs. Cover the dish and braise everything over medium heat for about 10 minutes.

3. Wash and clean the spinach and then scatter the leaves over the cooked vegetables. Sprinkle with lemon juice. Place the veal fillets on the spinach and sprinkle with olive oil.

4. Cover the dish again and braise everything again for another 5–7 minutes until the meat is tender. Arrange the vegetables on two plates together with the veal fillets. Season with salt and freshly ground pepper.

Two servings

30 minutes

6 potatoes
1 courgette
1 large onion
2 cloves garlic
a little fresh oregano
a little fresh thyme
250 ml (1/4 cup) vegetable stock
100 g (scant 4 oz) spinach leaves
1 tablespoon of lemon juice
two thin pieces of veal fillet, about 250 g (scant 9 oz) each
1 tablespoon olive oil
salt
freshly ground pepper

Rabbit fillet with Chinese Noodles and Mushrooms

Two servings

30 minutes

200 g (7 oz) Chinese
noodles
sea salt
1 tablespoon sunflower oil
250 g (9 oz) rabbit fillets
freshly ground pepper
4 spring onions (scallions)
1 ripe pear
1 mild red chilli pepper
100 g (3 1/2 oz) mixed
mushrooms
2 sprigs thyme

1. Put the noodles in a bowl and pour boiling salted water over them. Leave to stand briefly and drain. Heat the oil in a wok or deep pan and fry the rabbit for 6–8 minutes, turning the meat regularly. Season with salt and pepper, remove from the pan and keep warm.

2. Wash and prepare the spring onions (scallions) and cut into rings. Peel the pear, remove the core and dice finely. Cut the chilli lengthways, remove the seeds and cut into fine strips. Clean the mushrooms and cut into small pieces. Add the pear, spring onions (scallions), chilli and mushrooms to the cooking fat. Strip the thyme leaves from the stems and add to the pan. Cook this mixture for 8–10 minutes.

3. Cut the rabbit fillets into slices. Add them to the vegetables together with the noodles. Stir well and heat the mixture again. Season with salt and pepper and serve on two warmed plates.

Fried Asparagus with Smoked Loin of Pork

1. Peel the asparagus, remove the woody ends and cut diagonally into pieces of 1 cm / 3/8 in length. Peel and chop the shallots. Cut the meat into narrow strips. Blanch the tomatoes, peel, remove the stalks (stems) and chop coarsely.

2. Fry the asparagus pieces briskly in 2 table-spoons groundnut oil, add the chopped shallots and fry with the asparagus. Add the chicken stock a little at a time and boil away to reduce the amount of liquid. Season with salt, pepper and soya sauce and simmer for a little longer.

3. Fry the strips of pork in the rest of the oil. Arrange the asparagus on plates and serve with the strips of pork, chopped tomatoes and chervil.

Four servings

30 minutes

1.5 kg (3 lb) white asparagus
2 shallots
300 g (11 oz) smoked loin of pork
2 tomatoes
4 tablespoons groundnut oil
200 ml (7/8 cup) chicken stock
salt
freshly ground pepper
soya sauce
chervil as garnish

257

Kohlrabi Gratin with Wild Garlic Sauce

Two servings

30 minutes

3 kohlrabi
3 potatoes
250 ml / 8 fl oz (1 cup)
vegetable stock
salt
freshly ground pepper
some grated nutmeg
125 g / 4 1/2 oz (1/2 cup)
low-fat yoghurt (1.5%)
1 egg
1 bunch wild garlic
30 g (1 oz) low-fat hard
cheese
1 tablespoon sunflower
seeds

1. Peel the kohlrabi and potatoes and cut into slices 1 cm (3/8 in) thick. Heat the stock in a saucepan, add the potato and kohlrabi slices, cover and cook for about 15 minutes.

2. Remove the potatoes and kohlrabi from the water, drain well and place in a gratin dish. Season with salt, pepper and freshly grated nutmeg. Wash the wild garlic, chop finely and add together with the egg to the yoghurt. Stir well until smooth and pour over the vegetables.

3. Pre-heat the oven to 180 °C (350 °F), gas mark 4.

4. Grate the cheese and sprinkle with the sunflower seeds over the gratin. Bake in the oven for about 10 minutes.

Lamb Fillets with
Green Asparagus

258

1. Wash the asparagus, remove the woody ends and cut the asparagus stalks into pieces of 5 cm / 2 in length. Blanch the tomatoes in hot water, peel, remove the seeds and cut into small cubes.

2. Rinse the lamb fillets under cold water, wipe dry and cut into small pieces. Peel the shallots and the ginger. Chop both finely. Wash the chillies, cut lengthways, remove the stalk, the white pith inside and the seeds. Dice finely.

3. Heat 2 tablespoons olive oil, fry the asparagus for 2–3 minutes, add 125 ml / 4 fl oz (1 cup) water, cover and cook for 10 minutes until tender. Remove from the heat and stir in the tomatoes and chillies. Leave to stand for a while.

4. Heat the remaining oil and fry the lamb fillets for 5 minutes on each side. Add the chopped shallots and ginger and fry briefly. Add the wine. Add the asparagus to the meat. Season with salt and pepper and reduce a little to thicken the sauce.

Four servings

30 minutes

1 kg (2 1/4 lb) green asparagus
4 tomatoes
4 lamb fillets (about 100 g; 3 1/2 oz each)
2 shallots
1 small piece fresh ginger (about 1 cm; 3/8 in)
2 small chillies
4 tablespoons olive oil
125 ml (1/2 cup) dry white wine
salt
freshly ground pepper

259

Mussels with Wine and Tomato Sauce

Four servings
30 minutes

3 cloves garlic
5 spring onions (scallions)
1 leek
1/4 celeriac
1 carrot
5 tablespoons vegetable oil
1 sprig rosemary
1/2 teaspoon chopped thyme
1 large tin tomatoes (800 g; 1 3/4 lb)
2 kg (4 1/2 lb) mussels
500 ml (2 1/4 cups) dry white wine
salt
pepper
cayenne pepper

1. Peel the garlic and cut into thin slices. Peel the spring onions (scallions) and cut into thin strips. Cut the leeks into thin strips. Peel the celeriac and carrot. Cut the celeriac into small cubes and slice the carrots.

2. Heat the oil in a very large frying pan or saucepan. Add the prepared vegetables and fry briefly. Stir in the herbs and tomatoes with their juice. Simmer gently for about 15 minutes.

3. Wash the mussels carefully under the tap, using a brush. Throw away any mussels that are already open.

4. Add the wine to the tomato sauce and bring to the boil. Remove the rosemary and season the sauce with salt, pepper and cayenne pepper.

5. Add the mussels to the tomato sauce. Cover and cook over a high heat until ready. Shake the saucepan vigorously now and again. After about 10 minutes, serve the mussels and sauce on four warmed plates. Throw away any mussels that have remained closed during cooking.

Peppered Beef Fillet with Asparagus

1. Peel the asparagus, remove the woody ends and cook in boiling water with 1 tablespoon butter for 10 minutes until tender.

2. Season the slices of beef fillet generously with salt and coarsely ground pepper from the mill. Fry on both sides in the clarified butter.

3. Melt the butter, remove from the heat and let it cool down a little. Put the egg yolks in a bowl standing in a container filled with hot water and whisk vigorously, stir in the white wine and chopped parsley. Continue whisking until the mixture turns pale yellow and becomes foamy. Add the melted butter, first drop by drop, then stir in slowly until you obtain a smooth, creamy mixture. Season the sauce with salt, pepper and lemon juice.

4. Remove the asparagus from the water and drain. Arrange on the plates with the meat and serve with the hollandaise sauce.

Four servings

30 minutes

2 kg (4 1/2 lb) white asparagus
salt
15 g (1 tablespoon) butter
650 g (1 1/2 lb) sliced beef fillet
freshly ground pepper
15 g (1 tablespoon) clarified butter
250 g (1 1/4 cups) butter
yolks of 4 eggs
2 tablespoons medium dry white wine
2 tablespoons parsley
lemon juice

Beef Steak with Tomato and Cognac Sauce

Four servings

30 minutes

2 shallots
1/2 bunch chives
4 large tomatoes
1 tablespoon olive oil
15 g (1 tablespoon) butter
8 beef steaks (about 750 g;
1 3/4 lb)
salt
freshly ground pepper
3 tablespoons Cognac
1 tablespoon Worcester-
shire sauce
250 ml (1 cup) beef stock

1. Peel the shallots and cut into very thin slices. Wash the chives and chop finely. Pour hot water over the tomatoes. Peel, remove the stalks and chop coarsely.

2. Heat the olive oil and butter in a pan, season the steaks with salt and pepper and fry on both sides over a high heat, but do not overcook the meat. Remove from the pan and keep in a warm place.

3. Take the pan from the heat, pour away the excess fat, add the cognac, set light to it and return to the heat until the flames have died down. Soften the shallots in the pan. Add the tomatoes, Worcestershire sauce, beef stock , salt and pepper. Stir and bring to the boil.

4. Return the steaks to the frying pan and finish cooking. Arrange the steaks on a plate, reduce the sauce a little, add the chives and pour the sauce over the steaks.

Pork Fillet (Tenderloin) with Tomatoes

1. Wash the pork fillet, pat it dry and cut into strips or slices of similar size. Season generously with marjoram, lemon zest, caraway, salt and pepper.

2. Peel the garlic cloves, onions and spring onions (scallions). Chop the garlic finely and cut the onions and spring onions (scallions) into fine strips. Peel the tomatoes, cut into quarters and remove the seeds. Cut the tomato pieces into small cubes.

3. Heat the olive oil in a pan, add the garlic and fry. Add the pork and fry while turning the meat constantly. Remove the meat and garlic mixture from the pan and keep in a warm place.

4. Now add the onions and spring onions (scallions) to the cooking fat and fry until transparent. Add the tomatoes and cook briefly. Season the tomato mixture with salt, pepper, basil and oregano.

5. Arrange the pork fillet strips on four plates and garnish with the vegetables.

Four servings

30 minutes

800 g (1 3/4 lb) pork fillet
2 teaspoons chopped marjoram
1 teaspoon grated lemon peel
1/2 teaspoon ground caraway
salt
freshly ground pepper
4 cloves garlic
2 onions
8 spring onions (scallions)
8 tomatoes, chopped
2 tablespoons olive oil
4 tablespoons chopped basil
1 tablespoon chopped oregano

Sole with Leeks and Tomatoes

Four servings

30 minutes

500 g (18 oz) beef tomatoes
2 red onions
2 small leeks
2 tablespoons oil
salt
pepper
1 handful leaves of basil
1 kg (2 1/4 lb) sole
30 g (2 tablespoons) clarified butter

1. Peel the tomatoes, cut them into quarters and remove the seeds. Chop the tomato quarters into small cubes. Peel the onions and wash and clean the leeks. Cut both into thin rings.

2. Heat the oil in a pan and fry the onion and leek rings. Add the diced tomatoes and season with salt and pepper. Cook the leek and tomato mixture for about 10 minutes over low heat. Stir in the basil. Put the vegetable mixture in a warm place.

3. Remove the skin from the gutted soles and cut off the heads diagonally. Cut off the fins using scissors. Heat the clarified butter in a large pan, add the fillets of sole and fry on both sides until golden brown. Season with salt and pepper.

4. Arrange the fish fillets on a serving dish and garnish with the leek and tomato mixture.

Stuffed Sesame Pancakes (Crèpes)

1. Make a pancake (crepe) batter with the egg, flour, mineral water, a pinch of salt and sesame seeds. Cover and leave to stand for 10 minutes.

2. Drain the corn on the cob. Wash and prepare the pepper, sugar peas and cauliflower and cut into small pieces. Heat 1 teaspoon olive oil in a saucepan, add the vegetables and fry them. Pour in the stock and season with salt and pepper. Cover and simmer for about 10 minutes over a low heat.

3. For each pancake, heat one teaspoon olive oil in a non-stick frying pan and make the two pancakes, one after the other. Put the cooked vegetables on the pancakes, roll them up and arrange them on two warmed plates. Serve with the chilli sauce.

Two servings

30 minutes

1 egg
1 tablespoon spelt flour
4 tablespoons low-fat milk (1.5%)
3 tablespoons sparkling mineral water
sea salt
1 teaspoon sesame seeds
50 g (2 oz) small corn on the cob
1/2 red sweet pepper
50 g (2 oz) sugar peas
100 g (3 1/2 oz) cauliflower florets
3 teaspoons olive oil
freshly ground pepper
1 tablespoon vegetable stock
sweet-and-sour chilli sauce

265

Spaghetti with Cherry Tomatoes

Four servings

30 minutes

1 clove garlic
3 tablespoons olive oil
1 tablespoon chopped basil
1 tablespoon chopped parsley
500 g (18 oz) cherry tomatoes
spiced oil
herb salt
freshly ground pepper
500 g (18 oz) spaghetti
salt
150 g / 5 oz (1 cup) peas
150 g (5 oz) curd cheese with feta

1. Pre-heat the oven to 220 °C (425 °F), gas mark 7. Peel the garlic and chop finely. Stir the olive oil, garlic, basil and parsley together in a small bowl.

2. Put the tomatoes in a large baking tin and pour seasoned oil over them. Sprinkle with herb salt and pepper. Cook the tomatoes in the pre-heated oven for 10 minutes.

3. Boil the spaghetti in plenty of salted water following the instructions until cooked al dente. Add the peas 3 minutes before the end of the cooking time.

4. Drain the spaghetti and peas, reserving 250 ml / 8 fl oz (1 cup) of the cooking water in a bowl.

5. Stir the cooking water into the curd cheese and beat with a whisk to make a creamy sauce. Season to taste.

6. Add the mixture of spaghetti and peas to the cherry tomatoes in the baking tin. Pour the cheese sauce over it and stir well. Season again with salt and pepper and serve hot.

1. Peel the asparagus and remove the woody ends. Cook in boiling salted water with sugar and butter until done.

2. Cook the ravioli "al dente" in gently simmering lightly salted water.

3. Peel the shallots, dice and cook with the vinegar and pepper. Reduce to thicken the mixture. Add the stock .

4. Add 2 tablespoons water to the egg yolk and beat in a bain-marie until it becomes creamy. Add the shallot mixture, stir in the oil, add the tarragon and tomatoes and mix all the ingredients together. Season with salt and cayenne pepper. Heat carefully but do not bring to the boil.

5. Put the ravioli and asparagus in a large bowl or arrange on large plates and pour the sauce on top.

Four servings

30 minutes

1.5 kg (3 lb) white asparagus
salt
1 pinch sugar
10 g (2 teaspoons) butter
600 g (1 1/4 lb) fresh ravioli
with meat filling
1 shallot
6 tablespoons white wine-
vinegar
freshly ground pepper
4 tablespoons broth
yolks of 2 eggs
2 tablespoons olive oil
2 tablespoons tarragon,
finely chopped
3 tablespoons chopped
tomatoes
cayenne pepper

Honey Pancakes (Crèpes)

Two servings
30 minutes

60 g (1/2 cup) spelt flour
100 ml (1/2 cup) buttermilk
1 teaspoon thistle oil
2 eggs
1 pinch salt
1/2 teaspoon vanilla sugar
about 2 tablespoons honey
some cinnamon
icing (confectioner's) sugar

1. Put the spelt flour, buttermilk and thistle oil in a bowl and stir to make a smooth mixture.
2. Add the two eggs one after the other and beat the batter vigorously. Add the salt and vanilla sugar and stir. Leave the batter to stand for 25 minutes at least and stir again before the next stage.
3. Heat a non-stick pan and pour in about a quarter of the batter. Cook each pancake over a low heat for 2 minutes on each side until golden yellow. Remove from the pan and keep warm.
4. Spread some honey on the pancakes while they are still warm and sprinkle with cinnamon according to taste. Roll and sprinkle with icing (confectioner's) sugar.

Tuna and Celeriac with Pasta

1. Heat about 500 ml / 17 fl oz (2 1/4 cups) water in a large saucepan. Season with salt, add the pasta and cook following the instructions on the packet.

2. Peel the onion and chop finely. Heat the oil in a casserole and fry the onion until transparent. Peel the celeriac and cut into small cubes. Add to the casserole and season with a little grated nutmeg. Add the low-fat milk, cover and the cook the vegetables for about 10 minutes.

3. Drain the tuna, shred with a fork and add to the celeriac. Heat briefly. Season with salt and freshly ground pepper.

4. Wash the chives and chop finely. Drain the pasta and arrange on two plates, garnish with the vegetables and sprinkle the chives on top.

Four servings
30 minutes

200 g (7 oz) wholemeal
(wholewheat) pasta
salt
1 onion
1 teaspoon sunflower oil
1 small piece celeriac
some grated nutmeg
125 ml (1/2 cup) low-fat milk
(1.5%)
125 g (4 1/2 oz) tuna fish
without oil (from the tin)
freshly ground white pepper
1 bunch chives

Tuna with Celeriac

Two servings
30 minutes

salt
200 g (7 oz) wholemeal
noodles
1 onion
1 tablespoon sunflower oil
1 small celeriac
a little freshly grated nutmeg
125 ml / 4 fl oz (1/2 cup) milk
125 g / 4 1/2 oz (1/2 cup)
tuna without oil (tin)
freshly ground white pepper
1 Bunch chives

1. Bring approx. 1 1/2 litres / 49 fl oz (6 cups) of water in a large pan to the boil, salt, and add the noodles. Cook al dente according to the directions on the packet.

2. Peel and finely chop the onion. Heat the oil in a casserole, and gently fry the onion until transparent. Peel and dice the celeriac, add to the casserole and season with a little freshly ground nutmeg. Pour the low fat milk over the celeriac and cook with a lid for approx. 10 minutes.

3. Drain the tuna, flake with a fork, add to the celeriac, and briefly heat. Season with salt and freshly ground pepper.

4. Wash the chives and cut into little rolls. Portion the noodles onto two plates, add the celeriac mixture and sprinkle with chives.

1. Peel, quarter and core the apples. Grate the quarters finely.
2. Add lemon juice, mayonnaise and hazelnuts to the apples. Stir together until the consistency becomes creamy.
3. Add white wine to the cream shortly before serving and mix well.

Four servings
10 minutes

250 g (8 oz) apples
juice of 1/2 lemon
3 tablespoons mayonnaise
3 tablespoons roasted and grated hazelnuts (filberts)
20 ml (1 fl oz; 2 tablespoons) white wine

271 Gourmet Sauce

Four servings
10 minutes

250 g (8 oz) apples
juice of 1/2 lemon
100 g (scant 1/2 cup) mayonnaise
50 g (1/2 cup) finely chopped almonds
salt
freshly ground white pepper

1. Peel, quarter and core the apples. Grate the apple quarters and put into a bowl. Add the lemon juice and mix thoroughly.
2. Add the mayonnaise and almonds and mix well. Add salt and pepper to taste.

Whipped Apple Cream

Four servings
10 minutes

1 kg (2 1/4 lb) apples
6 leaves of gelatine
250 g (1 cup) sugar
1/2 sachet vanilla sugar

1. Peel, quarter and core the apples, then grate finely.

2. Dissolve the gelatine according to the instructions on the packet.

3. Put the grated apples into a bowl, add the sugar, vanilla sugar and the dissolved gelatine and beat until the consistency becomes foamy.

4. Use in the same way as whipped cream, with cakes, apple sauce or apple purée.

Suitable for almost all cakes and sweet biscuits.

1. Peel the tomatoes, cut into quarters and remove the seeds. Cut the tomato quarters into very small cubes. Peel the shallots and the garlic clove; chop finely. Coarsely chop the parsley. Cut the avocados in half lengthways, remove the stone and scoop out the flesh with a spoon; and into small cubes.

2. Mix all these ingredients together and season with chilli powder and lime juice. Stir the crème fraîche until smooth and add to the salsa.

May be used as a spread, or as a dip for savoury maize snacks or potato crisps.

Four servings
10 minutes

400 g (14 oz) plum tomatoes
2 shallots
1 clove garlic
1/2 bunch flat leaf parsley
1 avocado
salt
1/4 teaspoon chilli powder
juice of 1 lime
2 tablespoons crème fraîche

Tarragon Sauce

Four servings

10 minutes

2 eggs
juice of 1 lemon
450 ml / 15 fl oz (2 cups)
cream
4 teaspoons medium
strength mustard
4 tablespoons tarragon
vinegar
2 bunches tarragon
olive oil
salt
freshly ground pepper

1. Stir the eggs, lemon, cream, mustard and tarragon vinegar together. Add the finely chopped tarragon and olive oil. Season with salt and pepper.

Ideal for white fish or Asparagus dishes.

1. Peel the onion and garlic clove. Chop both finely. Peel the tomatoes, cut into quarters and remove the seeds. Cut the tomato quarters into small cubes.

2. Heat the oil in a pan. Add the chopped onion and garlic and fry. Add the diced tomatoes, honey, vinegar, salt and pepper and stir well. Cook the sauce until it thickens, stirring constantly.

3. Season the tomato and honey sauce with salt and pepper according to taste. Serve hot or cold.

A wounderful accompaniment to lamb chops, or as an alternative to cranberry jelly for baked camembert.

Four servings
10 minutes

1 small onion
1 clove garlic
8 medium tomatoes
3 tablespoons basil-infused oil
2 tablespoons forest honey
1 tablespoon balsamic vinegar
salt
pepper

Yoghurt and Herb Sauce

Four servings
10 minutes

6 tablespoons fresh herbs
2 small shallots
2 cloves garlic
3 cups full fat yoghurt
2 tablespoons olive oil
2 tablespoons balsamic vinegar
freshly ground pepper
salt

1. Wash and dry the herbs, and chop finely. Peel the shallots and chop finely. Peel and crush or press the garlic. Mix well and stir into a smooth sauce together with the other ingredients.

A sauce, suitable either for Asparagus dishes, or as a summer dip to accompany warm unleavened bread.

277

Cheese Dip

1. Mix the respective ingredients together, and season with the spices as given.

A wounderful dip for fresh white bread or crackers.

Four servings
10 minutes

200 g (7 oz) cream curd cheese
225 ml (1 cup) cream
salt
freshly ground pepper
1 teaspoon parsley, chopped
1 teaspoon chervil, chopped
1 teaspoon lemon balm, finely chopped

1. Stir the mustard, yoghurt and lemon juice together to make a smooth sauce. Season with salt and pepper and add the herbs.
2. Whip the cream until thick and stir into the herb sauce.

A most versatile sauce for meat or potato dishes.

Four servings

10 minutes

1 teaspoon mustard
125 g / 4 1/2 oz (1/2 cup) yoghurt
1 tablespoon lemon juice
salt
freshly ground pepper
2 tablespoons chopped herbs: parsley, chives, chervil, dill, green coriander (cilantro)
100 ml / 3 1/2 oz (scant 1/2 cup) cream

279
Olive and Egg Sauce

Four servings

10 minutes

2 hard-boiled eggs
2 tablespoons black olives, stoned
1 tablespoon fresh herbs
1 teaspoon capers
1 anchovy fillet
6 tablespoons olive oil
3 tablespoons white wine vinegar
freshly ground white pepper
salt

1. Shell the eggs and separate the whites from the yolks. Finely chop them, separately.
2. Chop the olives, herbs, capers and anchovey very finely. Stir in the oil and vinegar. Add the chopped egg yolks and egg whites. Season with salt and pepper.

Try this sauce with grilled fish.

Orange Dip

280

1. Mix the respective ingredients together, and season with the spices as given.

This sweet dip is ideal for parties when served with crackers.

Four servings

10 minutes

125 ml / 4 fl oz (1/2 cup) double (heavy) cream, whipped
3 tablespoons orange juice
1/2 teaspoon sugar
1 pinch salt
ginger, ground

1. Wash the spring onions prepare and cut into fine rings. Wash the tomatoes and cut into four. Cut the chillies in half, remove the stalks, the white pith inside and the seeds. Dice the bacon finely.

2. Melt 80 g/3 oz (6 tablespoons) butter, add the bacon and spring onions and fry lightly. Add the tomatoes and chillies and cook for another 5 minutes. Stir in the remaining butter.

Suitable for many pork dishes.

Four servings
10 minutes

8 spring onions (scallions)
12 small tomatoes
4 small chillies
400 g (14 oz) bacon
200 g (1 cup) butter

282 Devil's Dip

Four servings

10 minutes

100 g (3 1/2 oz) apples
100 g (scant 1/2 cup) tomato ketchup (catsup)
20 g (2 tablespoons) mustard
40 g (4 tablespoons) mayonnaise
juice of 1/2 lemon
salt
freshly ground black pepper
1/2 bunch chives

1. Peel, quarter and core the apples. Cut the quarters into fine julienne strips.
2. Put the apples into a bowl and add the tomato ketchup, mustard, mayonnaise and lemon juice. Stir well.
3. Season with salt and pepper. Wash the chives, snip into little rounds and stir in. Serve the sauce hot or cold.

Tomato Dip 283

1. Mix the respective ingredients together, and season with the spices as given.

A tasty dip for white bread or crisps.

Four servings

10 minutes

70 g (2 1/2 oz) tomato purée
3 tablespoons crème fraîche
juice of 1/2 lemon
salt
freshly ground pepper
1 pinch sugar

1. Cut the tomatoes in half, remove the seeds, cut into very fine strips and cut these in half again. Peel the shallots and cloves of garlic; chop finely.

2. Whisk the tarragon vinegar, mustard, sugar, salt and pepper together in a bowl. Slowly add the oil and stir it in. Add the tomatoes and stir well. Season again to taste.

Add a new touch to your lettuce for once!

Four servings
10 minutes

4 medium sized tomatoes
1 shallot
2 cloves garlic
125 ml (1 cup) tarragon vinegar
1/2 teaspoon medium strength mustard
1 pinch sugar
salt
white pepper
250 ml (1 cup) vegetable oil

285 White Wine Sauce

Four servings
10 minutes

50 ml (5 tablespoons) dry,
medium white wine
2 tablespoons medium
strength mustard
6 tablespoons mayonnaise
salt
cayenne pepper

1. Mix together wine, mustard and mayonnaise and stir until you obtain a smooth mixture. Season with salt and cayenne pepper.

This sauce tastes good with white meat dishes.

286

Tomato Stock

1. Peel the tomatoes and cut into small pieces. Put the chopped tomatoes into a stainless steel sieve. Press the tomatoes to extract all the liquid, catching the juice in a bowl.
2. Put the tomato juice in a small saucepan and simmer over a low heat without a lid until it begins to thicken a little.

Ca. 400 ml
15 minutes

1 kg (2 1/4 lb) over-ripe
tomatoes

Tomato and Onion Sauce

1. Peel the onions and cloves of garlic. Dice the onions. Peel the tomatoes, cut into quarters and remove the seeds. Dice the tomato quarters finely.

2. Heat the oil in a pan and braise the diced onions lightly. Add the tomatoes and simmer until the sauce begins to thicken, stirring constantly. Season with salt, pepper, vinegar and honey.

3. Shortly before the sauce is ready, add the pressed garlic. Season again according to taste. Serve the tomato and onion sauce hot.

Ideal for pork or jacket potatoes.

Four servings
15 minutes

5 red onions
1 clove garlic
800 g (1 3/4 lb) beef tomatoes
5 tablespoons olive oil
salt
black pepper from the mill
1 tablespoon apple vinegar
1 tablespoon honey

Tomato and Basil Sauce

Four servings
20 minutes

6 tomatoes
2 bunches of basil
3 shallots
15 g (1 tablespoon) butter
6 teaspoons sherry or white wine vinegar
60 ml (6 tablespoons) oil
375 ml (generous 1 1/2 cups) white wine
3 tablespoons lemon juice
salt
freshly ground pepper

1. Wash the tomatoes and cut in half. Chop the flesh finely. Wash the basil, dry and cut the leaves into thin strips.
2. Peel the shallots, dice finely and fry them in butter. Stir in the vinegar, oil, white wine and lemon juice. Bring to the boil and reduce the liquid to two-thirds. Stir the tomatoes and basil into the sauce and season with salt and pepper.

Serve this sauce with steamed vegetables and white bread.

1. Defrost the spinach, peel the onions and chop finely.

2. Melt the butter, add the onions and fry until transparent. Add the spinach and cook. Stir in the crème fraîche. Season with salt and pepper.

This sauces makes a good lunch when served with boiled or jacket potatoes.

Four servings

25 minutes

200 g / 7 oz (3/4 cup) creamed spinach, frozen
2 onions
25 g (2 tablespoons) butter
200 g / 7 oz (3/4 cup) crème fraîche
salt
freshly ground pepper

Tomato and Haricot (White) Bean Sauce

Four servings

25 minutes

600 g (1 1/4 lb) white beans from the glass
800 g (1 3/4 lb) beef tomatoes
3 shallots
1 clove garlic
150 g (5 oz) streaky bacon
1/2 bunch flat leaf parsley
2 tablespoons oil
salt
pepper

1. Drain the beans. Peel the tomatoes, cut into quarters and remove the seeds. Cut the tomato quarters into small cubes. Peel the shallots and clove of garlic and chop. Cut the streaky bacon into small pieces. Chop the parsley.
2. Heat the oil in a pan and sweat the bacon. Add the shallots and garlic. Fry until transparent. Add the haricot beans and diced tomatoes and cook to thicken the sauce for about 15 minutes, stirring constantly. Stir in the parsley and season with salt and pepper.
3. Serve the tomato and bean sauce hot.

An ideal accompaniment for all sorts of noodles.

Quark Sauce

1. Peel the onions, chop finely and sweat in 30 g / 1 oz (2 tablespoons) butter until transparent. Add the wine and vinegar and reduce the liquid to about one-third. Add the remaining butter and stir to incorporate it. Allow to cool.

2. Mix the quark and milk and stir until smooth. Stir in the tarragon. Season the sauce with salt, pepper and Worcestershire sauce.

A Sauce which may be served with fish or Asparagus dishes.

Four servings

30 minutes

1 small onion
60 g (4 tablespoons) butter
50 ml (5 tablespoons) dry white wine
50 ml (5 tablespoons) white wine-vinegar
100 g (3 1/2 oz) low fat curd cheese
100 ml (scant 1/2 cup) milk
1 tablespoon tarragon leaves, chopped
salt
freshly ground pepper
Worcestershire sauce

292

Hollandaise Sauce

Four servings
30 minutes

yolks of 4 eggs
2 teaspoons lemon juice
salt
freshly ground white pepper
250 g (1 1/4 cups) butter

1. Stir the egg yolks and lemon together, season with salt and pepper and whisk vigorously to obtain a creamy texture. Put in a bain-marie and stir over simmering water until it has thickened sufficiently. Add warm, melted butter a little at a time, whisking continuously.

Ideal for Asparagus dishes, but also for boiled or jacket potatoes.

293

Avocado Sauce

1. Heat up the milk, stir in the hollandaise sauce and bring to the boil.
2. Halve the avocados, remove the stones and scoop out the flesh with a spoon, mash and sprinkle with lemon juice
3. Stir the avocado purée into the hollandaise sauce and season with sugar and pepper.

Four servings
30 minutes

ingredients for hollandaise sauce (see recipe no. 292)
In addition:
250 ml / 8 fl oz (1 cup) milk
2 avocados
juice of 1 lemon
1 pinch sugar
freshly ground pepper

Basil-Flavoured Hollandaise Sauce

1. Make the hollandaise as shown in the recipe no. 292.
2. Stir in the tomato purée. Wash the lemon under running hot water, wipe dry, grate the zest and add more or less according to taste.
3. Wash the basil, dab dry, remove the leaves, cut into fine strips and add to the sauce.

Four servings
30 minutes

ingredients for hollandaise sauce (see recipe no. 292)
In addition:
1–2 tablespoons tomato purée
1 untreated lemon
fresh basil

Lime-Flavoured Hollandaise Sauce

Four servings
30 minutes

ingredients for hollandaise sauce (see recipe no. 292)
In addition:
1 untreated lime
freshly ground pepper

1. Make hollandaise sauce as shown in the recipe no. 292.
2. Wash the lime under running hot water, wipe dry and grate 1–2 teaspoons of zest. Stir into the hollandaise and season with pepper.

296

Truffle-based Hollandaise Sauce

Four servings
30 minutes

ingredients for hollandaise
sauce (see recipe no. 292)
In addition:
125 g / 4 1/2 oz (5/8 cup)
truffle butter
or some truffle oil

1. In the recipe for hollandaise sauce, page 122, replace half the butter—125 g / 4 1/2 oz (5/8 cup)—with truffle butter.
Or:
2. Make hollandaise sauce as shown in the recipe no. 292 and add a few drops of truffle oil to the sauce.

Walnut Hollandaise Sauce

297

1. Make hollandaise sauce as shown in the recipe no. 292.
2. Cut the butter into pieces and whisk into the sauce piece by piece. Chop the walnuts finely and stir into the sauce.

Four servings
30 minutes

ingredients for hollandaise
sauce (see recipe no. 292)
In addition:
80 g (6 tablespoons) butter
60 g (1/2 cup) walnuts

1. Peel the onions, chop them coarsely and sweat in the butter. Add 500 ml / 17 fl oz (2 1/4 cups) water or asparagus stock and bring to the boil, reducing the liquid by about half.

2. Stir in the cornflour and bring to the boil again. Stir in the mascarpone, lemon zest and lemon juice a little at a time. Heat again but do not boil. Season with salt, pepper and 1 pinch of sugar.

Steamed vegetables and rice can be transformed into a tasty main dish with this sauce.

Four servings

30 minutes

1 onion
20 g (1 1/2 tablespoons) butter
1 teaspoon cornflour (corn starch)
250 g (9 oz) mascarpone
juice and peel of 1 untreated lemon
salt
freshly ground pepper
1 pinch sugar

299 Tomato Sauce for Grilled Dishes

Six servings

30 minutes

2 tins of tomatoes (400 g; 14 oz each)
70 g (3 oz) red onions
4 pickled gherkins
5 tablespoons sunflower oil
2 teaspoons sugar
salt
pepper

1. Drain the tomatoes and cut into thin slices. Peel the onions and chop finely. Dice the pickled gherkins finely.
2. Heat the oil in a pan and braise the onions lightly. Add the tomatoes and gherkins. Season with sugar, salt and pepper. Cook the sauce until it begins to thicken, stirring constantly. Season again after cooking and leave to cool. Pour into screw-top jars and store in the refrigerator. The sauce should not be kept long.

Fresh Apple Compote

1. Peel, quarter and core the apples. Cut the quarters into small pieces.
2. Put sugar and 125 ml (1/2 cup) water in a pan and bring to the boil. Add the pieces of apple and the lemon juice and simmer until thick. Sweeten to taste.

Four servings
10 minutes

750 g (1 1/2 lb) apples
70 g (scant 1/3 cup) sugar
juice of 1 lemon

301 Apple Compote (Variation)

Four servings
10 minutes

750 g (1 1/2 lb) apples
peel from 1/2 untreated lemon
1 teaspoon cinnamon
70 g (scant 1/3 cup) sugar

1. Peel, quarter and core apples. Cut the quarters into small pieces.
2. Heat 125 ml/4 fl oz (1/2 cup) water in a pan. Add the pieces of apple, lemon peel, cinnamon and sugar. Cook everything on a low heat until soft. Sweeten to taste.

Tipsy Apple and Peach Salad

Four servings
10 minutes

550 g (1 1/4 lb) untreated apples
juice of 1 lemon
3 peaches
50 g (4 tablespoons) marzipan
1 tablespoon honey
6 tablespoons herb liqueur
6 tablespoons cream
100 g (1 cup) walnuts

1. Peel, quarter and core the apples. Cut into slices and put in a bowl. Sprinkle immediately with lemon juice and mix.
2. Wash the peaches, stone and cut into thin wedges. Add to the apples in the bowl and mix carefully.
3. Mix the marzipan with the honey, liqueur and cream. Stir into the fruit and fill small bowls with the salad. Chop the walnuts and sprinkle over the salad before serving.

1. Peel the banana and cut in half lengthways. Sprinkle with lemon juice. Pour some honey on a plate and roll the banana halves in it so that they are well coated.

2. Put the oats in a non-stick pan and fry until light brown without adding any fat. Lay the banana halves on the roasted oats and fry for a few minutes on the flat side first. Then turn the halves over very carefully so that the oats do not fall off and fry the other side.

3. Place the hot banana on two plates and sprinkle the remaining fried oats on top. Serve immediately.

Two servings
10 minutes

1 banana
1 teaspoon lemon juice
2 teaspoons honey
2 tablespoons oat flakes

Strawberries in Bilberry (Blueberry) Sauce

Two servings

10 minutes

125 g / 4 oz (1 cup) bilberries (blueberries)
1 tablespoon maple syrup
2 teaspoons port
200 g / 7 oz (1 1/4 cups) strawberries
a little icing (confectioner's) sugar
fresh mint leaves

1. Put the bilberries in a saucepan. Add the maple syrup and port. Bring to the boil while stirring and simmer over a low heat for 5 minutes until the berries burst, resulting in a thick sauce-like mixture.

2. Wash the strawberries, top and tail the fruit and cut in half. Arrange them on two pudding plates and pour the sauce over while still hot. Sprinkle icing (confectioner's) sugar on top and garnish with mint leaves.

Strawberry Quark

1. Wash the strawberries and remove the stalks. Cut them in half and arrange in two bowls.
2. Mix the milk and quark together until you obtain a smooth mixture and sweeten to taste with the maple syrup and grated orange zest. Pour this mixture over the strawberries.
3. Fry the oats in a non-stick pan without fat until pale brown and sprinkle over the strawberry quark.

Two servings
10 minutes

250 g / 9 oz (1 1/2 cups) fresh strawberries
200 g (7 oz) low-fat quark
2 tablespoons low-fat milk (1.5%)
1 tablespoon maple syrup
1 pinch grated untreated orange zest
2 tablespoons oat flakes

306 Baked Pineapple

Two servings
10 minutes

4 slices fresh pineapple (about 1 cm; 3/8 in thick)
2 tablespoons acacia honey
2 teaspoons white rum
2 teaspoons coconut milk

1. Cut the pineapple slices in half, place on a baking sheet covered with aluminium foil and sprinkle rum and acacia honey over them.
2. Pre-heat the oven to 180 °C (350 °F), gas mark 4.
3. Bake the pineapple in the oven for about 5–8 minutes. Arrange the pineapple pieces on two large plates and sprinkle with coconut milk while still hot.

307 Classic Semolina Pudding

Four servings
10 minutes

1/2 l (2 cups) milk
1 tablespoon butter
pinch of salt
50 g (scant 2 oz) semolina
1/2 teaspoon cinnamon
50 g (generous 3 table-
spoons) sugar

1. Heat milk and butter in a saucepan and bring to a boil. Pour in the semolina while stirring steadily and allow to cook for about 5 minutes.
2. Spoon the pudding into four small bowls, sprinkle with a mixture of cinnamon and sugar and serve.

Semolina with Apple Sauce 308

1. Prepare pudding as above and place in four small bowls. In the middle of each portion, make an indentation with a spoon and put a heaping spoon of apple sauce into it.

Four servings
10 minutes

Same ingredients as above plus 100 g (generous 1/3 cup) apple sauce

Bilberry (Blueberry) Yoghurt

1. Wash the bilberries and put a few to one side. Put the rest in a tall container with the maple syrup and a pinch of cinnamon. Purée with a hand-held mixer.

2. Using a whisk, stir the yoghurt into the bilberry purée. Pour into two small bowls and garnish with the reserved bilberries.

Two servings

10 minutes

100 g / 3 1/2 oz (5/8 cup) bilberries (blueberries)
2 teaspoons maple syrup
1 pinch cinnamon
250 g / 9 oz (1 cup) yoghurt

Quark Delight with Almonds

Two servings

10 minutes

250 g (9 oz) low-fat quark
2 tablespoons low-fat milk (1.5%)
1 tablespoon maple syrup
2 nectarines
1 tablespoon almonds

1. Mix together the milk and maple syrup. Put the quark into two pudding bowls.

2. Peel the nectarines, cut in half, remove the stones and cut into slices. Arrange the nectarine slices on top of the quark.

3. Coarsely chop the almonds, fry in a pan without fat and sprinkle over the quark and nectarine slices.

311

Sweet Couscous Maghrebine

Four servings
15 minutes

1/4 l (1 cup) water
4 tablespoons butter
a bit of salt
250 g (1 1/2 cups) couscous
100 g (scant 2/3 cup) raisins
5 tablespoons honey

1. Combine water, butter and salt in a pot and bring to the boil. Remove the pot from the heat and stir in the couscous together with the other ingredients. Cover and let rest for about 5 minutes, stirring the mixture with a fork once a minute.

Pear Compote

1. Put the cinnamon stick, cloves, lemon zest and maple syrup in a saucepan with 4 tablespoons of water and bring to the boil. Remove from the heat and allow to stand for a few minutes.

2. Peel the pears, cut into quarters, remove the cores and add to the mixture. Cover and simmer for about 5–8 minutes.

3. Remove the pears from the liquid and place them still lukewarm on two plates. Garnish each with a tablespoon of ricotta and sprinkle with flaked almonds.

Two servings

15 minutes

1 cinnamon stick
2 cloves
1 small piece untreated lemon zest
1 teaspoon maple syrup
2 pears
2 tablespoons ricotta cheese
1 teaspoon flaked (slivered) almonds

Figs in Red Wine and Blackberry Sauce

Two servings

15 minutes

125 g / 4 1/2 oz (1/2 cup) blackberries
125 ml / 4 fl oz (1/2 cup) red wine
1/2 teaspoon cornflour (corn starch)
1 tablespoon honey
3 fresh figs

1. Wash the blackberries and put a few aside as a garnish. Purée the rest with a hand-mixer. Pass the purée through a fine sieve into a saucepan.

2. Add the red wine and heat slowly. Mix the cornflour with 1 teaspoon water and stir until smooth. Add to the fruit purée and stir in carefully, making sure that there are no lumps. Bring briefly to the boil and sweeten with a tablespoon of honey.

3. Wash and prepare the figs and cut into slices. Arrange the fruit on two dessert plates and pour the hot red wine and blackberry sauce over it. Garnish with blackberries.

1. Break the spaghetti into pieces about 1 cm (1/2 inch) in length. Put the milk and butter in a pot and bring to a boil quickly. Add the spaghetti and, while stirring occasionally, let it cook for 10–15 minutes until tender. Stir in the vanilla extract.

2. Place the milk noodles into four small bowls. Mix cinnamon and sugar together and sprinkle over the noodles.

Four servings
15 minutes

150 g (generous 5 oz) spaghetti
1/2 l / 17 fl oz (2 cups) milk
1 tablespoon butter
2 drops vanilla extract
1/2 teaspoon cinnamon
2 tablespoons sugar

315 Apples with Custard

Four servings

20 minutes

650 g (1 1/2 lb) apples
50 g (1/4 cup) sugar
1 packet custard
8 sponge fingers
whipped cream to taste

1. Peel and cut the apples in half. Remove the cores. Dissolve the sugar in a saucepan with some water and add the apples. Cook until soft, but do not let the apples become too mushy.

2. Make the custard following the instructions on the packet.

3. Put the sponge fingers in a glass bowl. Arrange the apple halves on top.

4. Spoon the custard onto the apples. Decorate as desired with whipped cream.

Apple Fritters

1. Peel the apples and remove the cores carefully. Cut the apples into thick rings. Sprinkle with sugar and set aside.

2. Separate the eggs. Put flour, milk, egg yolk, oil and salt in a mixing bowl and mix to a smooth batter. Beat the egg whites until they are stiff and fold carefully into the batter.

3. Heat the fat in a large saucepan.

4. Dip the apple rings into the batter, turn them over to cover them completely and slip immediately into the hot fat. Cook to a golden brown.

5. Remove the fritters from the fat, drain on a kitchen towel and sprinkle with sugar.

Makes 12 fritters
20 minutes

650 g (1 1/2 lb) apples
2 tablespoons sugar
2 eggs
125 g (1 1/4 cups) plain (all purpose) flour
2 tablespoons milk
2 tablespoons oil
pinch of salt
fat for deep-frying

317 Beignets à la Princesse

Four servings

20 minutes

1.3 kg (2 1/2 lb) apples
2 teaspoons sugar
2 tablespoons rum
peel from 1/2 untreated lemon
125 g (1 1/4 cups) plain (all purpose) flour
2 eggs
pinch of salt
1 tablespoon oil
fat for deep-frying
1 packet custard

1. Peel the apples and core them. Cut into thick slices and put into a bowl. Add sugar, 1 tablespoon of rum and the lemon peel and stir carefully.

2. Separate the eggs. Mix flour, egg yolks and 200 ml / 7 fl oz (7/8 cup) water in a bowl and stir to a thick batter.

3. Add salt, oil and the rest of the rum to the batter and mix. Beat the egg whites until they form peaks and fold into the batter.

4. Heat the fat in a deep pan. Dip the slices of apple into the batter and deep-fry to a golden brown. Remove the apple rings from the fat and drain on kitchen paper.

5. Make the custard according to the instructions on the packet and serve with the beignets.

1. Peel, quarter and core the apples. Cut one third of them into fine slices and place in a shallow casserole. Pour over 40 ml / 2 fl oz (4 tablespoons) of white wine, 60 g / 2 oz (1/4 cup) sugar and 1 tablespoon of lemon juice. Cook over a medium heat until the apples are soft.

2. Cut the remaining apples into fine slices and put in a large saucepan. Add one-third of the lemon juice and 100 ml / 3 1/2 fl oz (scant 1/2 cup) water. Cook until soft. Line a sieve with kitchen towel, pour in the apple mixture and let it drain well.

3. Place the drained apple sauce in a bowl and mix with 120 g / 4 oz (1/2 cup) sugar, the rest of the lemon juice and 160 ml / 5 1/2 fl oz (3/4 cup) white wine. Spoon over the apples in the casserole.

4. Pour boiling water over the sultanas (golden raisins) and the currants and drain well. Sprinkle over the apples.

Four servings

25 minutes

500 g (1 lb) apples
200 ml (7/8 cup) white wine
180 g (3/4 cup) sugar
juice of 1 lemon
40 g (1/4 cup) sultanas
(golden raisins)
40 g (1/4 cup) currants

319

Apple and Vanilla Ice Cream

Four servings

25 minutes

500 g (1 lb) apples
4 scoops of vanilla ice cream
40 g (3/8 cup) cocoa
50 g (1/4 cup) sugar
125 ml (1/2 cup) condensed milk
1 teaspoon cornflour (corn starch)

1. Peel the apples, cut in half and remove the cores and. Put the apples in a saucepan with some water and cook briefly. Set aside.

2. In a small saucepan, stir the cocoa and sugar into the condensed milk and bring to the boil. Remove the pan from the heat and thicken the sauce with the cornflour.
Set aside to cool in the refrigerator.

3. Put the apples with the cut side uppermost in four small bowls. Fill each apple half with a scoop of ice cream.

4. Take the chocolate sauce out of the refrigerator and pour over the vanilla ice cream. Serve immediately.

Apple Temptation with Candied Flower Petals

1. Peel the apples, cut in half and remove the cores. Bring a saucepan of water to the boil and cook the apples until soft.

2. Remove the apple halves from the water and put into four small bowls, cut side down. Sprinkle with the chopped almonds.

3. Pour the apple juice into a saucepan with the salt and the sugar and bring to the boil. Stir some water into the cornflour and use it to thicken the apple juice. Remove the pan from the heat and stir the egg yolk carefully into the thickened apple juice. Gradually add the white wine.

4. Beat the egg whites until they form peaks and fold lightly and carefully into the apple juice mixture. Spread the zabaglione around the apples and garnish with the violets or rose petals.

Four servings
25 minutes

500 g (1 lb) apples
30 g (1/4 cup) chopped almonds
125 ml (1/2 cup) apple juice
pinch of salt
2 teaspoons sugar
1 tablespoon cornflour (corn starch)
1 egg yolk
250 ml (1 cup) white wine
some candied violets or rose petals

321 Banana Omelette

Two servings

25 minutes

2 eggs
50 g (scant 1/2 cup) icing
(confectioners) sugar
1 pinch salt
40 g (scant 1/2 cup) coarse
wholemeal (wholewheat)
flour
1/2 teaspoon baking
powder
2 tablespoons vanilla sugar
2 bananas
2 teaspoons low-fat quark
1 teaspoon semi-skimmed
milk (1.5 %)

1. Pre-heat the oven to 180 °C (350 °F), gas mark 4.

2. Separate the eggs. Beat the egg yolks in a bowl with half the icing sugar and two tablespoons of warm water to make a pale yellow foamy mixture. Add a pinch of salt to the egg whites and beat until stiff, then add the remaining sugar.

3. Add the beaten egg whites, flour and baking powder to the egg yolk mixture and fold in carefully. Line a baking sheet with greaseproof (waxed) paper. Put 4 balls of the mixture on the paper, leaving room between them, and flatten the tops slightly. Bake the omelettes in the oven for about 10–15 minutes until light brown.

4. Sprinkle vanilla sugar on a clean tea towel and turn the hot omelettes upside down onto it. Remove the greaseproof paper.

5. Peel the bananas and cut into slices. Mix the milk and quark and add to the banana slices. Fill the omelettes with the banana-quark mixture and serve immediately.

1. Wash the apples thoroughly. Remove the cores without cutting up the apples and slice off the top of each one.

2. Brush the lemon juice on the inside of the apples. Grease an ovenproof dish with butter. Place the apples in it and sprinkle with sugar.

3. Pre-heat oven to 200 °C (400 °F), gas mark 6.

4. Dice the ginger very finely and mix with the sultanas (golden raisins). Fill the apples with the mixture. Bake in the oven for 15 minutes on the middle shelf.

5. Take the apples out of the oven, pour the brandy over and set alight.

Four servings
25 minutes

500 g (1 lb) untreated apples
2 teaspoons lemon juice
softened butter for the dish
4 tablespoons sugar
2 pieces of ginger in syrup
2 tablespoons sultanas (golden raisins)
4 small glasses of brandy

323 Apple Confection

Four servings
30 minutes

200 g (7 oz) apples
150 g (2/3 cup) sugar
30 g (2 tablespoons)
candied lemon peel
100 g (3/4 cup) chopped
almonds
juice of 1 lemon
50 g (5 tablespoons) light-
coloured jam (jelly)
small rice wafers.

1. Peel, quarter and core the apples. Cut the quarters into small pieces.
2. Heat 125 ml / 4 fl oz (1/2 cup) water in a saucepan. Add the sugar and the apples. Cook until they are on the point of disintegrating.
3. Cut up the lemon peel and mix into the apple sauce together with the chopped almonds, the lemon juice and the jam (jelly).
4. Pre-heat the oven to 150 °C (300 °F), gas mark 2.
5. Scoop out small amounts of the mixture with a teaspoon and drop onto the wafers. Line a baking tray with greaseproof paper, put the wafers on it and allow to dry in the warm oven.
6. Remove the wafers from the oven and cool on a wire rack.

1. Peel the apples and remove the cores carefully. Put them in a casserole and sprinkle with lemon juice and 4 tablespoons of sugar. Add 125 ml / 4 fl oz (1/2 cup) water and cook the apples.

2. Remove the apples from the heat and place on a plate. Crumble the sponge into a bowl. Add the cranberry preserve and almonds and mix. Fill the apples with this mixture.

3. Stir the milk, custard powder, remaining sugar, butter and egg yolks in a bowl over a pan of hot water until the mixture is of a smooth, creamy consistency. Set aside to cool.

4. Wash and sort the cranberries. Once the cream has cooled, pour over the apples and garnish with the cranberries.

Four servings

30 minutes

4 apples
juice of 1 lemon
50 g (1/4 cup) sugar
100 g (3 1/2 oz) sponge fingers
150 g (scant 1/2 cup) cranberry preserve
50 g (1/2 cup) chopped almonds
250 ml (1 cup) milk
1/2 packet custard
20 g (3/4 oz) butter
2 egg yolks
20 g (1/8 cup) fresh cranberries

Apples in Mulled Wine

Two servings

30 minutes

2 sachets mulled wine
spices (including cinnamon
and cloves)
125 ml / 4 fl oz (1/2 cup)
red wine
2 apples
2 teaspoons maple syrup

1. Bring 125 ml / 4 fl oz (1/2 cup) water to the boil in a small saucepan. Add the mulled wine spices and the red wine and simmer over a low heat for about 10 minutes for the flavours to develop. Remove the sachets of spices.

2. Peel and core the apples and add whole to the wine mixture. Cover and simmer over a low heat for about 15 minutes.

3. Arrange the braised apples on two plates, add the maple syrup to the mulled wine and reduce briefly over a high heat. Pour the sauce over the apples and serve immediately.

Umm Ali (Ali's Mother)

1. Bake the puff pastry in the oven for about 10 minutes according to the directions on the package or until it begins to brown. Remove it and cut up coarsely with a knife.

2. In the meantime bring the milk and sugar to a boil. Then pour about 1/4 of the mixture into oven-proof dessert bowls. Add a quarter of the coconut flakes, raisins and chopped peanuts as well as the pieces of pastry. Then add another quarter of the milk and the other ingredients and so on, until everything has been used up.

3. Top each portion with a litle cream. Place the bowls in the oven pre-heated to 200 °C (400 °F), gas mark 6, and bake until the Umm Ali begins to turn golden.

Four servings
30 minutes

4 slabs of frozen puff pastry or strudel dough
1/2 l / 17 fl oz (2 cups) milk
50 g (3 1/2 tablespoons) sugar
3 tablespoons coconut flakes
2 tablespoons raisins
2 tablespoons chopped peanuts
100 ml / 3 1/2 fl oz (generous 1/3 cup) heavy cream

327 Apple-beer Punch

Makes 1 litre
10 minutes

500 g (1 lb) apples
juice of 1 lemon
150 g (2/3 cup) sugar
2 cloves
cinnamon
1 untreated lemon
600 ml (2 1/2 cups) beer

1. Peel, quarter and core the apples. Cut the quarters into thin slices.
2. Stir the sugar, cloves and cinnamon into the lemon juice. Put in a pan with the apple slices and bring briefly to the boil. Take the pan off the stove and set aside to cool.
3. Wash the lemon thoroughly and cut into slices. Mix the cooled apple mixture with the beer and lemon slices and serve ice cold.

Apple Vinegar Drink

1. Mix the apple vinegar with the buckthorn juice and the honey.
2. Add the mineral water and serve chilled.

Makes 1 litre
5 minutes

2 tablespoons apple vinegar
1 tablespoon buckthorn juice
1 teaspoon honey
1 litre (4 1/2 cups) mineral water

329

Apple and Bilberry (Blueberry) Drink

Makes 1 litre
5 minutes

500 g (1 lb) untreated apples
2 tablespoons bilberries (blueberries)
1 untreated lemon
juice of 1/2 lemon

1. Wash the apples thoroughly and cut into quarters. Wash and pick over the bilberries (blueberries).
2. Press the apples and the bilberries in a juicer, add lemon juice to taste and pour into glasses.
3. Wash the lemon well and cut into eighths. Put a wedge of lemon on the edge of each glass.

330 Grapefruit and Coconut Juice

Makes 1 glass
10 minutes

1 grapefruit
juice of 1/2 lime
1 teaspoon honey
2 tablespoons coconut milk
1 teaspoon grated coconut

1. Halve the grapefruit and squeeze the juice. Mix the grapefruit juice with the juice of half a lime and the coconut milk, sweeten with honey and sprinkle with grated coconut.

331

Banana Shake with Almond Paste

1. Cut up the bananas and blend in the food processor with 1 cup of milk and the almond paste. Add the rest of the milk a little at a time. On hot days, serve with ice cubes.

Four servings
10 minutes

1 l (4 cups) milk
6 bananas
5 tablespoons almond paste

Apple Milkshake

1. Wash the apples thoroughly, remove the cores and quarter. Cut one of the quarters into thin slices and set aside for the decoration.
2. Put the milk in a blender. Add the apple quarters, egg yolks and honey. Blend thoroughly.
3. Pour the apple milkshake into tall glasses and garnish with the reserved apple slices.

Makes 1 litre
10 minutes

1 kg (2 1/4 lb) untreated apples
1 litre (4 1/2 cups) milk
4 egg yolks
8 tablespoons honey

Tomato Juice

Makes 4 glasses
10 minutes

2 kg (4 1/2 lb) ripe beef tomatoes
1 teaspoon Italian herbs
2 tablespoons honey
2 pinches cardamom
salt
pepper

1. Peel tomatoes, remove seeds and cut into small pieces. Put tomatoes in a liquidizer, add 2 tablespoons of water and purée at highest speed until the mixture has turned into juice.
2. Season the tomato juice to taste with herbs, honey, cardamom, salt and pepper. Pour into a jug, cover with clingfilm and cool in the refrigerator. Use within 24 hours.

334

Ice-cold Lime and Tomato Tea

Makes 4 glasses
10 minutes

8 ice cubes
400 ml (1 3/4 cups) cold green tea
200 ml (7/8 cup) vegetable juice
200 ml (7/8 cup) tomato juice
salt
pepper
Tabasco
2 tablespoons lime juice

1. Wrap ice cubes in a tea towel and crush with a hammer. Put the crushed ice cubes in four longdrink glasses.
2. Mix the vegetable and tomato juice with the green tea; season with salt, pepper, tabasco and lime juice. Pour the the lime and tomato tea into the glasses and serve immediately.

Bloody Mary

335

1. Put the ice cubes in four longdrink glasses.
2. Stir the vodka and lime juice into the tomato juice; season with ground paprika, salt, pepper and a dash of tabasco.
3. Pour the Bloody Mary over the ice cubes and garnish each glass with a slice of lime. Serve immediately.

Makes 4 glasses
10 minutes

12 ice cubes
600 ml (2 1/2 cups) tomato juice
80 ml (3/8 cup) vodka
4 tablespoons lime juice
paprika
salt
white pepper
Tabasco
4 lime slices

1. Peel the papaya and mango, remove the stone and cut the flesh into small cubes.
2. Cut the orange in half and squeeze the juice . Pour the orange juice, cubed papaya and mango into the liquidizer and purée.
3. Season the fruit drink with a pinch of cinnamon, dilute to taste with mineral water and pour into a large glass.

Makes 1 glass
10 minutes

1/2 papaya
1/2 mango
1 orange
pinch cinnamon
sparkling mineral water

337

Mango Buttermilk

Makes 1 glass

10 minutes

1 ripe mango
1/2 banana
300 ml (1 1/4 cups) buttermilk
1 teaspoon orange juice
1 pinch ground ginger

1. Peel the mangos and banana. Remove the stone and cut the mango into slices, putting two slices aside for the garnish. Put the diced mango and banana in the liquidizer and purée.

2. Add the puréed fruit to the buttermilk and stir well. Season with orange juice and ground ginger and pour into a large glass. Garnish with the slices of mango.

Cucumber and Red Pepper Drink

1. Peel the cucumber, remove the seeds and cut into cubes. Wash the pepper, remove the stalk and seeds, and chop. Put the vegetables in the liquidizer, then pass through a fine sieve.

2. Peel the garlic, press it through a garlic press and add to the puréed vegetables. Stir in the yoghurt—and mineral water to taste—and whisk vigorously. Season the drink with sea salt, freshly ground pepper and finely chopped dill.

Makes 1 glass
10 minutes

200 g (7 oz) cucumber
1 red sweet pepper
1/2 clove garlic
100 g / 3 1/2 oz (3/8 cup) yoghurt
sparkling mineral water
sea salt
freshly ground pepper
1 teaspoon chopped dill

Carrot and Orange Drink

Makes 1 glass
10 minutes

1 orange
150 ml (5/8 cup) carrot juice
pinch cinnamon
1 teaspoon honey
1/2 teaspoon cream

1. Peel the orange, cut in half, cut off one slice and put to one side. Squeeze the rest of the orange.
2. Mix the orange juice with the carrot juice, stir in the cream and season with a pinch of cinnamon and honey. Pour into a large glass and garnish with the slice of orange.

Citrus Fruit Cocktail

340

1. Mix together the freshly squeezed orange and grapefruit juice and add the pineapple juice. Season with freshly ground ginger and pour into a glass with ice cubes.
2. Cut the carambola (star fruit) into slices, make a notch in each slice and slip onto the edge of the glass as decoration.

Makes 1 glass
10 minutes

juice of 1 grapefruit
juice of 1 orange
200 ml (7/8 cup) unsweet-
ened pineapple juice
pinch ground ginger
ice cubes
1/2 carambola (star fruit)

Pear and Banana Shake **341**

1. Peel the banana and the pear. Remove the core from the pear. Cut the pear and the banana into pieces and purée with the milk in the liquidizer. Pour the milk shake into a large glass and sprinkle with grated chocolate.

Makes 1 glass
10 minutes

1 banana
1 pear
250 ml (1 cup) low-fat milk (1.5%)
1 teaspoon grated chocolate

342 Peach-Banana Shake

Makes 1 glass
10 minutes

1 banana
1 peach
250 ml (1 cup) milk
1 teaspoon raisins

1. Peel the banana and remove the stone from the peach. Cut the fruit into pieces and blend in the food processor with the milk and raisins. Pour the milk shake into a large glass.

343

Beetroot and Carrot Drink

Makes 1 glass

10 minutes

200 ml (7/8 cup) beetroot juice
200 ml (7/8 cup) carrot juice
1 teaspoon sour cream
freshly ground pepper
1 small piece horseradish
a few parsley leaves

1. Mix together the beetroot juice, carrot juice and sour cream. Stir well and season with freshly ground pepper.

2. Peel some horseradish, grate finely and add to the mixed juices. Wash the parsley, chop the leaves finely and sprinkle on the juice.

344

Green Tea Drink

1. Bring about 250 ml / 8 fl oz (1 cup) water to the boil, remove from the heat and leave to cool a little. Put two tea bags in a pre-heated teapot and pour the hot water on top, allow to brew for about 3 minutes.

2. Season the green tea with lime juice and ground ginger. Sweeten with honey according to taste.

Makes 1 glass

10 minutes

1 tea bag green tea
1 tea bag peppermint tea
1 teaspoon lime juice
pinch ground ginger
1 teaspoon honey

Peach and Kiwi Fruit Milkshake

1. Peel the peach and kiwi fruit, remove the peach stone and cut both fruits into eight pieces. Put in a tall container, add a pinch of vanilla sugar and a tablespoon of sour milk, and purée with a hand-held electric mixer.
2. Add the puréed fruit to the rest of the sour milk and stir well. If the milk-shake is too thick, add some more sour milkor skimmed milk. Pour into a tall glass and sprinkle with chopped hazelnuts.

Makes 1 glass
10 minutes

1 peach
1 kiwi fruit
1 pinch vanilla sugar
125 ml (1/2 cup) low-fat
sour milk
a little skimmed milk
1 teaspoon chopped
hazelnuts

346 Cinnamon and Honey Flavoured Cocoa

Makes 1 glass
10 minutes

200 ml / 7 fl oz (7/8 cup) milk
1 teaspoon cocoa powder
1 pinch cinnamon
1 pinch ground cardamom
1 teaspoon honey
1 teaspoon chocolate flakes

1. Heat up the milk, add the cocoa powder and stir until it is dissolved. Bring the cocoa briefly to the boil.

2. Season the cocoa with a pinch of cinnamon and cardamom and sweeten with honey to taste. Pour the hot cocoa into a mug and garnish with chocolate flakes.

Hazelnut Milk Drink 347

1. Grind the hazelnuts finely. Put in a tall container, add the yoghurt and stir vigorously with a small whisk.

2. Sweeten the milk-shake to taste with honey and vanilla sugar.

Makes 1 glass
10 minutes

1 tablespoon shelled hazelnuts
100 g / 3 1/2 oz (3/8 cup) yoghurt
200 ml (7/8 cup) milk
1 teaspoon honey
1/2 teaspoon vanilla sugar

Spiced Tomato Cocktail

1. Wash the tomatoes, remove the stalks, chop into pieces, purée and pass through a fine sieve.

2. Add the chopped chives and stir in the sour milk. Season with chilli powder and lemon juice. Dilute with mineral water according to taste.

Makes 1 glass
10 minutes

200 g (7 oz) tomatoes
1 teaspoon chives
1 tablespoon low-fat sour milk
1 pinch chilli pepper
lemon juice
sparkling mineral water

349 Nectarine Shake with Wheat Germ

Makes 1 glass
10 minutes

2 nectarines
300 ml (1 1/4 cups) buttermilk
1 teaspoon maple syrup
1 tablespoon wheat germ

1. Peel the nectarines, cut them in half, remove the stones and purée in the liquidizer.

2. Add the buttermilk and stir well. Sweeten the nectarine shake with maple syrup, pour into a tall glass and sprinkle wheat germ on top.

350 Avocado and Kefir Drink

Makes 1 glass
10 minutes

1/2 ripe avocado
1 teaspoon lemon juice
150 ml / 6 fl oz (5/8 cup) kefir
freshly ground white pepper
1 teaspoon chives

1. Scoop out the flesh of the avocado pear with a spoon. Sprinkle with lemon juice and purée in the liquidizer.
2. Add the kefir and stir well. Season the avocado and kefir drink with freshly ground pepper. Pour into a glass and sprinkle the chopped chives on top.

Strawberry Buttermilk Drink

351

1. Wash the strawberries. Remove the stalks and any blemishes. Purée with the maple syrup and grated lemon zest. Mix the strawberry purée and buttermilk together.
2. Pour the strawberry buttermilk drink into a tall glass, sprinkle with grated coconut and garnish with lemon balm.

Makes 1 glass
10 minutes

200 g / 7 oz (1 1/4 cup) strawberries
1 tablespoon maple syrup
1/2 teaspoon grated untreated lemon zest
125 ml / 4 fl oz (1/2 cup) buttermilk
1 teaspoon grated coconut
a few leaves lemon balm

Watermelon Drink

1. Peel the watermelon and remove the seeds, cut into cubes and put in a tall mixing bowl. Purée the watermelon with a hand-held electric mixer. Season with a pinch of ground ginger, a little vanilla sugar and lemon juice.
2. Dilute the puréed melon with mineral water or Prosecco. Pour into a tall glass and garnish with mint leaves.

Makes 1 glass
10 minutes

1 piece watermelon (about 200 g; 7 oz)
ground ginger
1/2 teaspoon vanilla sugar
1 teaspoon lemon juice
125 ml / 6 fl oz (1/2 cup) sparkling mineral water or Prosecco (or other sparkling white wine)
a few mint leaves

353 Blackcurrant and Lemon Kefir

Makes 1 glass
10 minutes

100 ml (1/2 cup) blackcur-rant juice
1 tablespoon lemon juice
1 tablespoon rosehip purée
200 ml (7/8 cup) kefir
1 pinch cinnamon

1. Mix the blackcurrant juice, lemon juice and rosehip pulp together. Add the kefir, stir well and season with a pinch of cinnamon.

Lassi with Sugar

Four servings
10 minutes

400 g / 14 oz (1 2 /3 cups) yoghurt
400 ml / 14 fl oz (1 2 /3 cups) carbonated mineral water
3 teaspoons sugar

1. Blend all the ingredients. In summer, serve with ice cubes.

355

Mint-Yoghurt Lassi

1. Blend all the ingredients. In summer, serve with ice cubes.

Four servings
10 minutes

500 g / 17 oz (2 cups) yoghurt
300 ml / 10 fl oz (1 1/4 cups) carbonated mineral water
1 tablespoon dried mint
pinch of salt

Oriental Mint Yoghurt Drink—Fruity Variation

1. Mix all the ingredients well. In summer, serve with ice cubes.

Four servings
10 minutes

Ingredients as above, but use 300 ml / 10 fl oz (1 1/4 cups) of yoghurt instead of 500 ml / 17 fl oz (2 cups).
plus:
200 g / 7 oz (1 1/4 cups) strawberries, blended
juice of 1/2 lemon

357 Hibiscus Tea

Bring water to the boil in a pot. Add the hibiscus flowers and simmer for 10 minutes. Pour in 4 tea cups and sweeten to taste. Serve hot or cold.

Four servings
10 minutes

1/2 l / 17 fl oz (2 cups) water
2 tablespoons hibiscus flowers
4 teaspoons sugar

358 Oriental Black Tea with Mint

Four servings
10 minutes

1/2 l (2 cups) water
4 teaspoons black tea
3/4 teaspoon dried peppermint leaves
4 teaspoons sugar

1. Bring water to a boil. Pour over the tea and let brew for 3 minutes.
2. After about a minute add the peppermint leaves to the tea pot. Add the sugar, stir and serve the tea in small Turkish tea glasses.

Oriental Black Tea with Mint—North African Variation

359

1. Prepare the tea as in the previous recipe. Add the pignoli to the tea shortly before serving.

Four servings
10 minutes

Ingredients as in the previous recipe with:
4 teaspoons pignoli

Oriental Coffee

1. In a small saucepan mix the water with the coffee, cardamom and sugar and boil up the mixture several times. Pour the coffee into mocha cups and serve.

Four servings
10 minutes

200 ml (3/4 cup) water
4 teaspoons coffee
pinch of cardamom
2–4 teaspoons sugar (to taste)

361 Oriental Café au Lait (Milk Coffee)

Four servings
10 minutes

Ingredients as in the previous recipe plus:
600 ml (generous 2 1/3 cups) milk

1. Prepare the coffee as in the previous recipe. Pour into four heatproof glasses.
2. Heat the milk and pour into the coffee. Stir and serve.

362 Apple-peel Tea

Makes 1 litre
15 minutes

200 g (7 oz) apple peel
sugar or honey to taste
1 untreated apple

1. Pour 1 l (4 1/2 cups) cold water in a saucepan, add the apple-peel and boil for 10 minutes. Strain through a sieve into a jug.
2. Wash the apple thoroughly and peel it so that the peel comes off in a long spiral. Add sugar or honey to taste and use some of the spiral apple peel as a garnish.

Winter Punch 363

1. Heat about 300 ml (1 1/4 cups) water in a small saucepan. Add the cloves, cardamom and cinnamon stick. Bring briefly to the boil. Suspend the tea bag in the saucepan, cover and simmer for about 10 minutes over a low heat.
2. Remove the tea bag, cinnamon stick and cloves from the liquid. Add the orange and lemon juice. Heat the punch but do not boil. Sweeten with honey according to taste and serve hot.

Makes 1 glass
15 minutes

1 cinnamon stick
3 cloves
1 pinch ground cardamom
1 tea bag mallow tea
juice of 1 orange
juice of 1 lemon
1 teaspoon honey

Apple Water

1. Wash the apples thoroughly, cut into eighths and remove the cores.
2. Bring 1 1/2 litres water to the boil in a large saucepan. Add cinnamon, lemon peel and apples and cook for about 15 minutes until the apples are soft. Line a sieve with cheesecloth, tip in the apples and drain into a jug.
3. Sweeten the apple water with sugar or honey and leave to cool. Serve chilled.

Makes 1 litre
20 minutes

1.5 kg (3 lb) untreated apples
cinnamon
peel from 1 untreated lemon
sugar or honey

365 Pepper and Celery Drink

Makes 1 glass
30 minutes

100 ml (1/2 cup) whey
200 ml (7/8 cup) celery juice
100 ml (1/2 cup) red pepper juice
1 pinch chilli pepper
grated nutmeg
1/2 bunch chives

1. Pour the whey into an ice-cube tray and put in the freezer.
2. Stir the celery and red pepper juice together. Season with chilli powder and a pinch of grated nutmeg.
3. Wash and dry the chives, and chop finely. Remove the tray with iced whey cubes, put them in a large glass, pour in the juice and sprinkle with the chopped chives.